SCENES FROM THE

RAILWAYS IN AND

STAFFORD

Stafford. 3rd March 1933. "Royal Scot" Class locomotive No.**6166** *London Rifle Brigade* approaches the station with an Up express, preparing for the 30 mph restriction that faces it through Trent Valley Junction. On the left of the engine is the former No.1 loco shed that was removed in the late 1930s. Further to the left is former No.2 shed, which was later modernised. To the right is the "bank" engine or station pilot probably a "Precursor" Class 4-4-0 tank.

E.R. Morten.

EDWARD TALBOT

Designed and Edited by Gregory K. Fox
Typeset by Bill Rear, Johnstown, Wrexham
Printed by the Amadeus Press, Huddersfield

Published by Foxline Publishing
32, Urwick Road, Romiley, Stockport. SK6 3JS

Acknowledgements

In compiling this book, I have enjoyed the help of many friends, fellow enthusiasts and local historians. In particular, Ken Wood, a former fireman at Stafford shed, and keen enthusiast of the steam era, has gone to great pains to help with information and photographs. Others who have given help freely and generously in various ways have been: Don Adnitt, Joan Anslow, Don Best, John B. Bucknall, Harold Frogatt, Phil Jones, Terry Mountford, G. N. Nowell-Gosling, Professor F. M. Page, L. W. Reader, Eric Russell, F. W. Shuttleworth and Peter J. Stead. To all of them, and to the photographers who have contributed their work, I offer my grateful thanks.

The photographs are credited individually, except for those taken by photographers now unknown (those from the Roger Carpenter collection are believed to have been taken by T. Hinkley). None of the photographers will object, I am sure, if I single out one of them, Percy Kendrick, for special mention. Some years ago, after I had admired some of his pictures, he very kindly allowed me to have prints made from his negatives. He covered the Stafford area particularly well in the period from the mid 1920s to the late 1940s. He was using a medium telephoto lens to excellent effect long before such lenses became commonplace.

He also told me about his friend, W. W. Hollis, who used to live in Wolverhampton Road, Stafford, was employed by the LNWR at Crewe and died before the Second World War. His fine photographs regularly appeared in The Railway Magazine. Sadly his relatives are believed to have been persuaded by the fire authorities in the early part of the war that his collection of negatives was a fire risk and destroyed them. If any readers have information about them, or about anything else in this book, I would be delighted to hear from them.

Edward Talbot
Stafford
January 1994

The crew of Stanier '8F' 2-8-0 No.**48294** posing for the camera with the GPO sorting office in the background; they have just come off the shed and are waiting for the road to the up sidings. The driver, on the left, is my father, who like me was always known as Ted Talbot; on the right is a fireman he worked with regularly for a time and got on with particularly well, Dave Beattie. *Edward Talbot.*

Contents

Enginemen continued to be employed at Stafford after the shed was closed. They were needed to drive the diesel shunters used for station pilot work and the electric and diesel multiple units used for local passenger trains. These duties were gradually reduced until in 1984 train crew ceased to be employed at Stafford. To commemorate the final demise of Stafford as a locomotive depot, the enamel badge reproduced here was produced on the initiative of driver G. F. Perks. It features a 'Prince of Wales' class engine, as spanning the LNWR, LMS and BR periods, and depicts Stafford castle in the top left-hand corner and the LMS shed code 5C in the right. The dates below are 1838, when the first shed was opened (six months after the opening of the Grand Junction, though an engine was possibly stationed before that) and 1984, when the last train crew were dispensed with.

View of the exterior of the station, taken probably from the balcony of the North Western Hotel, later the Station Hotel, on 11th May 1915, when in the words of The Staffordshire Advertiser 'the grim realities of this deadly decimation and disastrous war were brought home to the people of Stafford'. A special ambulance train carrying soldiers wounded at Ypres, many of them Canadians, left thirty for Stafford General Hospital before continuing to Manchester. Stretcher cases were moved in four LNWR vans, one of which, horse-drawn, is backed up in the station entrance. Walking wounded were taken in various vehicles including Councillor Bailey's car in the centre and a Lotus Shoes van on the right, lent by Edward Bostock, the firm's proprietor. The station master attempted to avoid a crowd outside and ordered strict silence but every vehicle was loudly cheered as it left for the hospital.

Chronology of the Railways in and around Stafford

1837 4th July. Grand Junction Railway opened from Curzon Street, Birmingham, to Newton Junction. Stafford station built north of Newport Road. Bridges over line at Newport Road and Wolverhampton Road.

1838 Six months after opening, engine shed built at Stafford.

1843-4 New Stafford station in Elizabethan style, built by John Cunningham of Liverpool.

1845 Grand Junction Railway absorbed Liverpool & Manchester Railway.

1846 London & North Western Railway formed by amalgamation of London & Birmingham Railway, Grand Junction Railway and Manchester & Birmingham Railway.

1847 26th July. Opening ceremony of Trent Valley Railway (leased to LNWR).
15th September. Trent Valley line opened for limited traffic Rugby to Stafford.
1st December. Trent Valley line fully opened.

1848 North Staffordshire Railway line from Stoke on Trent via Stone to Norton Bridge opened.

1849 Stafford-Wellington line opened by Shropshire Union Railways & Canals Company (leased to LNWR).
1st May. North Staffordshire Railway line from Stone to Colwich opened.

1859 7th November. Cannock Mineral Railway line from Cannock to Rugeley opened (leased by LNWR).

1861-2 New Stafford station built in Italian style by John Parnell of Rugby to design of W. Baker, LNWR architect. Engine shed for Southern Division and lodge for enginemen built at same time by same contractor.

1866 North Western Railway Hotel built in Italian style to design of Robert Griffiths of Stafford.

1867 23rd December. Stafford & Uttoxeter Railway opened.

1874 1st July. Stafford Common station opened.

1876 Stafford-Crewe line quadrupled. New station at Great Bridgeford.
1st August. LNWR began working passenger trains between Colwich and Macclesfield.

1877 Milford & Brocton opened for passenger traffic and level crossing replaced by overbridge.

1881 1st August. Stafford & Uttoxeter Railway taken over by the Great Northern Railway.
1st August. Spread Eagle station renamed Gailey.

1882 22nd January. Milford & Brocton opened for goods traffic.

1884 Down platform at Stafford made into an island platform with scissors crossing in centre of new platform.

1887-9 Roofing extended over island platform and bays at both ends.

1898 Milford & Brocton-Stafford section quadrupled.

1899 8th December. Serious accident to 'Irish Mail' at Norton Bridge.

1903 Rugeley-Colwich section quadrupled.

1914 29th March. Armitage-Rugeley section quadrupled.

1923 1st January. Grouping of the railways; LNWR and GNR became part of the London Midland & Scottish Railway and London & North Eastern Railway respectively.

1932 Serious accident at Great Bridgeford.

1939 4th December. Passenger services ceased on Stafford -Uttoxeter line.

1948 1st January. Railways nationalised with title of British Railways.

1949 8th August. Great Bridgeford closed to passengers.

1950 6th March. Milford & Brocton closed to passengers.

1951 5th March. Goods services ceased between Stafford and Uttoxeter; line from Stafford to Air Ministry sidings remained open, closed on to Bromshall Junction.
18th June. Gailey closed to all traffic.

1952 4th February. Standon Bridge and Whitmore closed to passengers.
Great Bridgeford station demolished.

1954 New Stafford No. 5 signal box opened. Many LNWR gantries removed and replaced.

1957 23rd March. 'Final Run' by SLS special on Stafford -Uttoxeter line.

1959 15th June. Four Ashes closed to passengers.
22nd June. Great Bridgeford closed to all traffic.

1959 October. Track lifted on Stafford-Uttoxeter line.

1960 7th March. Milford & Brocton closed to goods traffic.
May. Coffee Tavern at Stafford station closed.

1961 May. Demolition of Stafford station begun.
June. Work on building new station begun.

1962 1st December. Electric power switched on between Stafford and Crewe.
31st December. New Stafford station officially opened by Councillor Rees Tyler, Mayor of Stafford, a signalman in No. 5 box.

1963 7th January. Electric haulage of service trains between Stafford and Liverpool/Manchester begun.

1964 September. Stafford-Shrewsbury passenger trains withdrawn.

1965 19th July. Stafford shed closed.

1966 6th August. Stafford-Newport line closed (lifted by August 1967). Goods traffic to Newport worked from Wellington.

1968 6th January. Serious accident at Hixon.
Stafford Common closed to freight. Private siding to RAF 16MU still open.

1969 Newport-Donnington line closed and lifted.

1972 Station Hotel demolished.

1973 Stafford Common station demolished.

1975 November. Last freight train to RAF 16MU.

Railways in and around
STAFFORD

Historical Survey

Stafford was one of the earliest towns in the country to enjoy the benefits of a railway service. This came about simply by virtue of its geographical location rather than because of any great traffic the town might produce. To the north, the Liverpool & Manchester Railway, the first main-line railway in the world, had opened in 1830. To the south, a railway was projected between Birmingham, the centre of the growing manufacturing region of the Black Country, and London. Birmingham businessmen also wanted a rail link with Lancashire and especially with the port of Liverpool. In addition to serving their interests, this line would provide a through route between the other two companies. It was named appropriately the Grand Junction Railway and was opened on 4th July 1837.

The route chosen for the Grand Junction was as obvious as the need for the line itself. At its northern end it formed a junction with the Liverpool & Manchester Railway at Newton Junction. This point was chosen because it was roughly the same distance from both Liverpool and Manchester. The station took its name from the nearby town of Newton le Willows. From Newton Junction the Grand Junction line headed directly south through Warrington and across Cheshire and Staffordshire. A station was built at Crewe, as it was intended to be a junction, but at the time the site was surrounded by open countryside. South of Warrington the only town of any note was Stafford. From there the line veered slightly to the south west so as to serve Wolverhampton and then to the south east so as to approach Birmingham from the east. This was necessary in order to connect with the London & Birmingham Railway at Curzon Street.

In the early days of railways engineers were concerned to avoid steep gradients, because of the difficulties they presented to the early steam locomotives. Fortunately for the Grand Junction the terrain through which it passed was not steeply graded. The hardest climbing occurred between Stafford and Crewe, the summit being at Whitmore. Trains coming south faced the steepest gradients as far as Madeley, after which the bank eased slightly. Going north from Stafford the climbing was more even.

The point is sometimes made nowadays that British Rail is handicapped in trying to achieve higher speeds because railways were pioneered in this country. That may be true as regards certain curves and the loading gauge; but it is equally true that the railways today still benefit because the pioneers chose the easiest gradients and moreover built the line to last. Many of the original Grand Junction structures such as bridges and viaducts are still in use to this day, despite the greatly increased speeds and loads. An example is the viaduct at Penkridge constructed originally by Brindley.

At the main points on the line, Birmingham, Wolverhampton, Stafford, Whitmore, Crewe, Hartford and Warrington, the Grand Junction built 'first-class' stations. These were stations where only 'first class' trains stopped and from which connecting road services ran to surrounding districts. The intermediate stations were designated 'second class'. Between Wolverhampton and Crewe there were second-class stations at Four Ashes, Spread Eagle, Penkridge, Bridgeford, Norton Bridge and Madeley. Spread Eagle was renamed Gailey in 1881. Its original name was taken from an inn near the junction of the Watling Street with the Stafford-Wolverhampton road, where one of the same name still stands today.

In the event, the opening of the Grand Junction Railway preceded that of the London & Birmingham, which opened only as far as Boxmoor on 20th July 1837. Completion through to Birmingham was delayed by the construction of Kilsby tunnel south of Rugby, where the workings were inundated by underground water which had not been expected. Eventually the difficulties were overcome and the whole line was opened on 17th September 1838.

At Curzon Street both railways had their own terminal stations alongside each other. No provision for through running had been made in planning the layout, and interchange of traffic involved much shunting and consequently much delay. Initially, this probably seemed acceptable but very soon, as traffic increased, the working of trains at Curzon Street became a difficult and often lengthy process.

Thus it soon became clear that a more direct link between London and the north was desirable and the Rugby & Stafford Railway was proposed as early as 1839. It was supported by the main towns on the route, Nuneaton, Tamworth, Lichfield and Rugeley, but was at first opposed by the two companies it aimed to serve. They regarded each other as rivals rather than allies, and both supported schemes which the other saw as threatening its interests. Eventually, the Trent Valley Railway, its revised title, was incorporated by Act of Parliament in 1845.

Before the construction of the Trent Valley line was completed, it became part of the London & North Western Railway, which was formed on 16th July 1846 by the merger of three major companies: the London & Birmingham Railway, which had taken control of the Trent Valley line very soon after its authorisation in 1845; the Grand Junction Railway, which had absorbed the Liverpool & Manchester in 1845; and the Manchester & Birmingham Railway, which had opened from Manchester to Crewe on 10th August 1842.

The opening ceremony of the Trent Valley took place on 26th July 1847 but additional work on bridges near Stafford delayed the opening to through traffic until 1st December 1847. No major works were needed in its construction and the gradients were easy throughout. The only feature of note was at Stafford where to bring the Trent Valley line into the Grand Junction south of the station a long and severe curve through almost ninety degrees was necessary at Queensville.

Today it is very easy for anyone standing near Trent Valley Junction at Stafford, perhaps watching trains from the Wolverhampton Road overbridge, to imagine that the main London line was the first railway through Stafford. Its four tracks sweeping away to the south round the curve seem far more important than the two tracks veering off towards Wolverhampton. The course of the Grand Junction line, however, is a long and gentle curve from south of the junction right through the yard and station to beyond the first overbridge to the north. This, and the sharp curve on the main line, is clear evidence that it was built first.

An attractive feature of the Trent Valley line was its distinctive buildings designed by William James Livock. Fortunately a few of them still survive today. The most notable is the restored station building on the up side at Atherstone. Another is on the down side at Colwich - it is believed to have been the original station building but is now a house - and there are two former crossing keepers' cottages, both also now houses, one south of Atherstone and one south of Nuneaton, both on the down side.

Very soon after the LNWR came into existence, its system in the Stafford area was complete. In 1847 it leased the Shropshire Union Railways & Canals Company, partly as a defensive measure against expansion by the Great Western Railway. The Shropshire Union proposed converting several of its canals into railways and building some new ones. Only one of the latter was completed, the Shrewsbury to Stafford line, the section from Wellington to Stafford being completed in 1849.

While the LNWR system had been expanding in the south and centre of the county of Staffordshire, similar developments had been taking place in the north and east around Stoke on Trent. The Railway Mania of 1845 had produced a host of schemes; out of them came the North Staffordshire Railway and the first lines serving the Potteries. The North Stafford line from Stoke to Norton Bridge was opened in 1848, giving access to Stafford, Birmingham and the south, and the whole of its main line from Macclesfield to Colwich in 1849. This provided the North Stafford with a direct link from Stoke to Euston and also served as an alternative route between Manchester and Euston to that via Crewe. Later, when the branch from Cannock to Rugeley Trent Valley was opened, on 7th November 1859, it provided a useful link for local services, both passenger and goods, between the Potteries and the West Midlands.

The last new line to be built in the Stafford area was the Stafford & Uttoxeter Railway which opened on 23rd December 1867. It was very unusual if not unique in that it did not own a station at either of end of its line, the two places that gave it its name. At Stafford it used the LNWR station and at Uttoxeter the North Staffordshire station, which it reached by running powers from Bromshall Junction. Eventually, on 1st July 1874, it opened its own station at Stafford Common, which then became its headquarters, but its passenger services still started and terminated as before. It survived

as an independent company until 1st August 1881 when it was taken over by the Great Northern Railway and so became the western extremity of its through route from Nottingham via Derby Friargate. The original Grand Junction station of 1837 did not last long. It was replaced in 1843-4 by a new station designed in the Elizabethan style by John Cunningham of Liverpool. This station was probably intended at the time to be permanent but it was soon found to be quite inadequate. There were probably two reasons for this. Firstly, the LNWR directors decided in 1860 that Stafford was to be the border station between its Northern and Southern divisions. This caused a considerable increase in activity at Stafford, since among other things engines had to be changed on all trains passing from one division to the other. Secondly, in the twenty years since the previous station had been planned, traffic had expanded rapidly to a level which had not been expected. Indeed, the railways in general and the LNWR in particular continued to expand right up to the end of the First World War.

The new station was much larger and was built to the north of the previous one in 1861-2. It was designed in the Italian style by the LNWR's own architect, W. Baker, and the contract for its construction was awarded to John Parnell of Rugby. The new layout essentially had two main platforms with through lines in the centre, the up platform being numbered 1 and the down 2. At the ends of both platforms were bay platforms for local passenger trains and for parcel, mail and carriage traffic. The passenger entrance was on the east side and there were goods lines on the west side, 'round the back' of the down platform, which also gave access to the engine shed.

At the same time Parnell also built a new engine shed for the Southern Division alongside the Northern Division shed, and probably also the 'lodge' for enginemen working to Stafford from other sheds. A little later the North Western Railway Hotel was built near the station entrance.

At its north end the Trent Valley line required a severe curve to bring it round the south of Stafford to join the Grand Junction line from Birmingham. Here, the 2pm 'Corridor' negotiates Queensville curve in 1899 (in fact, most probably it has stopped for the photograph to be taken). The engine is the most famous of all the Webb compounds, No. 1304 *Jeanie Deans*. It achieved a remarkable record for working the train punctually, despite the fact that it regularly had the sizeable load seen in this picture, weighing well over 300 tons. The train is approaching the spot where the public footbridge seen in the following picture, known locally as the Crinoline Bridge, still crosses the line. *British Rail.*

increasing traffic at this time began to cause considerable delays north of Stafford. The line to Crewe had only two tracks on which to handle the traffic for both the Birmingham and Trent Valley lines. Goods trains had to be shunted into sidings at intermediate stations out of the way of the faster-moving passenger trains. Consequently, work was begun on converting this section to four tracks, to allow fast and slow trains to be separated. It was finally completed in 1876.

Soon afterwards, in the early 1880s, it was found necessary to increase capacity at the station further. A through platform was built on the west side of the down platform, converting it into an island platform, and numbered 3. At first it seems to have been used as an up platform, and there also seems to have been a short down platform to the west of the goods lines, which was probably reached by means of a boarded crossing. In 1884, however, the Board of Trade agreed to the use of a scissors crossing in the centre of platform 3, enabling it to be used by trains in either direction, and the short platform was then done away with. This was the first occasion that a scissors crossing was used in this way and once approved by the Board of Trade it set a precedent on the LNWR. Soon several other stations such as Rugby, Crewe and Stockport had similar arrangements. Later in the 1880s, the roofing on the down platform was extended over the west side of the island platform.

Once the LNWR system was developed, regular traffic flows became established. So far as long-distance passenger traffic was concerned, many of them were much the same as they are today. Express services were provided on the main lines through Stafford linking the major cities in the south, London and Birmingham, with the north, Liverpool, Manchester, Scotland, North Wales, and the north of England. In providing these through services, much use was made of through carriages which were attached and detached at junctions as required. This is a feature which has disappeared from the modern timetable.

Local passenger services were provided on all routes from Stafford and were timed to suit hours of work and events such as market days and bank holidays. They provided the only means of easy transport for people living in country areas. Thus wayside stations were built at close intervals along all lines. Stopping services were provided on many routes which no longer exist today. For example, some Birmingham trains started at Silverdale near Newcastle-under-Lyme; from Wolverhampton some took the direct route via the Stour Valley line and others went via Bescot and Aston; there were also trains between Stafford and Walsall via Rugeley and Cannock, and Stafford and Coventry via Nuneaton.

Two centres that were of great importance on the LNWR system have now declined, so far as traffic through Stafford is concerned. One was the Holyhead route, which was much more important than it is now, as Ireland was governed from London and rapid communication was vital. As Stafford is roughly half way between London and Holyhead, it was the ideal place at which to change engines, and this may well have been a major factor in the decision to make Stafford the change-over point between the Northern and Southern Divisions.

The other major centre was Leeds, which was an integral part of the LNWR system, having services to Crewe via Stalybridge and Stockport, as well as direct services to Liverpool. There were, of course, no Leeds expresses running through Stafford; but express goods services were provided between the West Riding and both London and Birmingham. They were very smartly worked as they were in competition with the Midland Railway and also, so far as London was concerned, with the Great Northern Railway.

Perhaps the greatest changes, compared with the present day, have occurred in goods traffic. Until the growth of road transport after the First World War, the economic life of the country depended on the railways for transport. Except for a small amount of goods transported by canal, every commodity went by rail, small consignments of a perishable nature, such as butter, milk, meat and fish, manufactured goods of every kind, and large tonnages of coal and minerals.

'Princess Royal' class Pacific No.**46207** *Princess Arthur of Connaught* restarting a Euston-Liverpool express on 15th August 1960. On the right a Stanier class '5' with a Down goods waits for the signal to clear. In steam days, especially in the 1940s and early 1950s it was quite common for a queue of goods trains, perhaps four or five, to be held up here on the Down Slow line. The section was 'permissive', meaning that the absolute block regulations did not apply and a train was permitted to advance slowly up to the rear of the one in front. It was often difficult to find an opportunity for them to cross the Birmingham line at Trent Valley Junction and also if they were due to shunt in Salop Sidings, there was often no room to take them. *Edward Talbot.*

Every village shop depended on the railway for supplies and every wayside station was served at least once a day by pick-up goods trains from the nearest railway centre. This applied as much to the Stafford area as it did to anywhere in the country. In addition, much through goods traffic passed through the station, and much shunting went on in the yards, which were rarely if ever quiet.

Operations on the Stafford-Shrewsbury line are a good example of the consequences of competition among the pre-grouping companies. Originally, the line was little more than a branch off the LNWR main line but eventually, as the railway system to the west and south of Shrewsbury developed, it became increasingly important. Firstly, the LNWR acquired, jointly with the Great Western, the Shrewsbury & Hereford Railway, and so gained access to South Wales, Bristol and the West of England. Then it took over the Central Wales line, which gave it access to Swansea and West Wales. At Shrewsbury also it made connection with the Cambrian Railway and the Great Western.

Thus Stafford became the point where goods traffic between all places on the LNWR system to the south and all places served via Shrewsbury was re-marshalled. Regular goods services from London and Birmingham, for example, arrived in Salop Sidings on the down side and corresponding services from Shrewsbury were dealt with in the sidings on the up side. A well known regular traffic was beer from Burton to South Wales, which reached Stafford via Wichnor Junction and Lichfield Low Level - no doubt, the brewers patronised the LNWR to help keep the Midland Railway's rates at acceptable levels! Regular flows of traffic such as these were supplemented by any other traffic the company's agents could obtain. So any business obtained by the LNWR goods agents in Nottingham or Leicester, for example, was sent via Stafford and Shrewsbury, even though much more direct routes existed by other companies. The Burton beer traffic was retained by the railway for many years and was only switched to the Midland route in the mid 1960s to allow the Stafford-Shrewsbury line to be closed.

There were equally complicated arrangements for passenger traffic. Through services were provided between both London and Birmingham, and destinations reached via Shrewsbury, and Stafford was responsible for the re-marshalling of the through carriages. For example, in 1910 the 1.40pm from Stafford to Shrewsbury conveyed portions from London to Aberystwyth, Barmouth and Swansea, and from Birmingham to Aberystwyth and Swansea. The London carriages arrived on the 11am from Euston, which left a through carriage for Buxton at Nuneaton and also conveyed two 65ft dining cars as far as Stafford, one first class only and the other second and third class. The carriages from Birmingham arrived on the 12.10pm from New Street, which conveyed sections for Keswick and Blackpool. The main-line trains were broken up or remarshalled on arrival at Stafford, their through carriages being detached and other vehicles added; then the through carriages from both trains had to be remarshalled into the correct order to form the 1.40pm departure to Shrewsbury. Similarly, in the reverse direction an arriving train from Shrewsbury would be broken up and its through carriages attached to services for London and Birmingham. All these activities involved complicated shunting, and the platform staff and the shunters, as well as the station pilot engines, were kept busy. Through services between Euston and Swansea continued to be provided in LMS days but ceased by the Second World War and were never resumed afterwards.

In 1923 the grouping of the various railway companies into four large companies took place. The LNWR and GNR ceased to exist, being absorbed into the London Midland & Scottish Railway and London & North Eastern Railway respectively. Thus, despite the change, Stafford still had two rival companies. In 1948 the four companies were nationalised and British Railways was formed. For some seventy years, right through the LMS period, Stafford station itself remained virtually unaltered, so that even in the late 1940s and early 1950s it was much the same as in the nineteenth century. Even then the main changes were minor and mainly concerned signalling. Many of the wooden posts and gantries of the old LNWR signals had begun to rot underground and needed to be renewed. The signals at the north end of the station were altered first. No. 5 signal box, which was then on the up side just south of Bagnall's bridge, was replaced by the present No. 5 box on the down side in 1954. The signals it controlled were replaced either by colour lights or by LMS upper quadrant semaphores on steel posts and gantries. Subsequently, other LNWR signals in the area were replaced also. Other minor changes were slight modifications to the track layout and removal of sidings.

Thus the 1860s station, as modified in the 1880s, survived largely unaltered until May 1960, when demolition work began in preparation for electrification. The present station was officially opened on 31st December 1962, though it had been in use a fortnight earlier. Most appropriately, the opening ceremony was performed by Rees Tyler, a signalman in No. 5 box and who was then Mayor of Stafford.

View looking north along platform 1, showing a drinking fountain made of red granite and dated 1864 on 7th January 1960; beyond it is a standard LNWR station seat with 'STAFFORD' carved in the back. When the old station was demolished, publicity at the time stated that the drinking fountain would be incorporated in the new station but this was never done and it was presumably destroyed

Four Ashes

An unidentified Webb tank engine leaving the station with a local passenger train to Wolverhampton about 1900. *Bernard Matthews collection.*

This view of Four Ashes, looking towards Stafford, taken on 28th November 1961, shows the main station buildings on the Down side, over two years after closure to passengers (15th June 1959). The platform elevation of this Grand Junction station however belies the fact that it was built on three levels, with station master's accommodation in the "house" to the right of the Booking Office. The signal box was a standard LNWR structure of the period (1875) with an anticipated life expectancy in 1910 of twenty five years! Directly opposite the box was a small goods yard with a capacity for 15 wagons, and a Lie Bye Siding for 53 wagons, reflecting the need for such a facility for goods trains, this being approximately the mid-point between Stafford and Wolverhampton on what was essentially a route for quicker-moving trains. *British Railways*

This rear elevation of Four Ashes station, taken on 28th November 1961, again after closure, shows the three storeyed outline, almost in original condition save for the modified low level window/door combination. Today the cottages still stand alongside the railway although there is little evidence to show that a station existed. The brick overbridge was replaced by a reinforced concrete span prior to the line's electrification.
British Railways.

Close up of the Grand Junction station building at Four Ashes, only discoloured spaces on the wall indicating lack of use of the place. Traditional LNWR features are still prominent with the wall mounted oil-lamps, cast iron Booking Office sign, and timber hut, a later addition to the scene (note earlier picture). Taken on 28th November 1961. *British Railways.*

General view of the down platform at Gailey, taken from the Watling Street overbridge looking towards Wolverhampton, on 16th June 1951, the last day of passenger service.
F. W. Shuttleworth.

The Up platform at Gailey on the same occasion as the previous picture, photographed looking towards Stafford, with the Watling Street (A5) overbridge on the left. *F. W. Shuttleworth.*

The last train to call at Gailey, a local hauled by 'Patriot' Class 4-6-0 No.**45520** *Llandudno* comprising four coaches, about to depart at 7.06pm. The service was the 6.24pm ex Birmingham New Street to Stafford but contained through carriages for Manchester London Road.
F.W. Shuttleworth.

Gailey

Penkridge

'Royal Scot' class 4-6-0 No.**6102** *Black Watch* south of the station with an express from Glasgow to Birmingham in the mid 1930s. The contrast between the three tall signals on the left and the small one on the right is striking. This photograph was taken with a medium telephoto lens, which has 'brought up' the background, showing an LNWR 'Super D' shunting in the yard beyond the bridge.   *P. S. Kendrick*

Another view taken on the same occasion as the previous photograph. LMS 'Crab' 2-6-0 No.**13111** pulls away from the station with an Up express, probably a relief to the Glasgow-Birmingham express. The shed plate reads '10', Aston.   *P. S. Kendrick.*

Penkridge

Penkridge was another station built on an embankment some five miles south of Stafford. This turn of the century view shows low platforms and a foot crossing, a situation which today would be "somewhat frowned upon". A small goods yard was situated approximately half a mile away on the Up side north of the station. Facilities almost mirrored Four Ashes but in this instance a Lie Bye Siding for 63 wagon units was located on the Down side serving northbound trains.   *Bernard Matthews collection.*

An up goods leaving Stafford on the Wolverhampton line in the early 1930s. The engine is the former LNWR 'Experiment' *Glendower* and in its day was one of the most famous engines on the line, being allocated to Camden for working the 'Corridor' between Euston and Crewe. Here it carries LMS No.**5466**. About 1930 Camden's 'Experiments' were transferred to Stoke shed and were regularly used on the Stoke-Bushbury goods. With the kind of loads seen here, they still more than earned their keep.

P. S. Kendrick

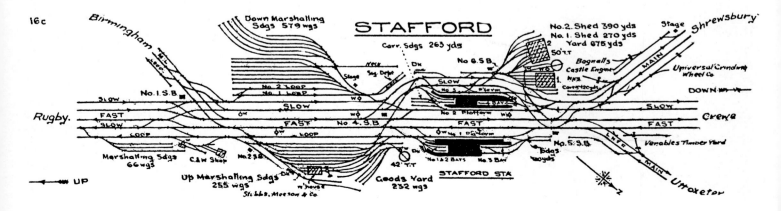

LMS compound 4-4-0 No.1154 approaching with a Down express in the mid 1930s. On the left is Rugeley No. 1 signal box and on the right the branch goes off to Rugeley Town, Hednesford and Walsall. *P. S. Kendrick.*

Midland '3F' class 0-6-0 No.3410 standing on the Down Hednesford line by Rugeley No. 1 signal box about 1930. *P. S. Kendrick.*

A 'Super D', LMS No.**9031**, coming off the branch at with a train of coal from the Cannock Chase pits in April 1947.   *P. S. Kendrick.*

Stanier class '3P' 2-6-2 tank No.**103** leaving with a local passenger train to Rugeley Town and Walsall. The junction with the main line is to the rear of the train - Rugeley No. 1 signal box is in the distance on the extreme left of the picture. In the left foreground is the turntable, while on the right, beyond the cutting, can be seen the tall signals controlling the southern approach to Rugeley on the main line. Another train is due off the branch; it is signalled to take the line round the back of Trent Valley station.

P. S. Kendrick.

Rugeley Trent Valley

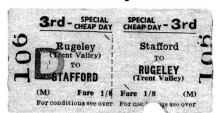

An early view, about 1885, of the station, looking roughly south from the Down side to the buildings on the Up side. The platforms were staggered, the Down platform being out of the picture to the left.   *Bernard Matthews collection.*

A later view, about 1900, before work on the widening had begun. Again the photograph is taken looking south, from the end of the Down platform.
Bernard Matthews collection.

Another view of **Rugeley Trent Valley** about 1900, showing the main building from a wider angle.   *L&GRP No.2403.*

General view, looking south from the footbridge. The date is 1947 but the scene would have been much the same at any time after the widening of the Armitage-Colwich section of the main line. This took place in two stages. The four tracks between Rugeley and Colwich came into use in 1903 and those between Rugeley and Armitage on 29th March 1914.   *P. S. Kendrick.*

View looking north from the footbridge on the same occasion as the previous picture.
P. S. Kendrick.

View from the same footbridge as the previous picture but slightly more to the left in the mid 1950s. The LNWR wooden signal posts have been replaced by steel posts and a standard BR maroon and white station nameboard has been erected on the Up platform but essentially the layout remains the same.   *H. C. Casserley.*

Rugeley Trent Valley

An Up goods running through the station on the fast line about 1936. The engine is Stanier 2-6-0 No.**13267**.   *P. S. Kendrick.*

An Up Trent Valley local passenger train standing in the station in the early 1930s. The engine is a Bowen Cooke 'Superheater Tank', LMS No.**6992**, and is allocated to Stafford shed.   *P. S. Kendrick.*

The section between Rugeley Trent Valley and Colwich was a favourite haunt of lineside photographers, probably because it was easily accessible by road as well as on foot from either station. Here the Up 'Coronation Scot' speeds towards Rugeley in July 1937 behind 'Coronation' class Pacific No.**6223** *Princess Alice*.   *P. S. Kendrick.*

Another famous engine in the same location. The first of the 'Royal Scots', No.**6100** *Royal Scot*, hard at work on an up express in the mid 1930s.   *P. S. Kendrick.*

The 'Royal Train' en route from Liverpool to Euston on 20th March 1937, hauled by the last two 'Jubilees', No.**5741** *Leinster* and **5742** *Connaught*. At the request of King George V the 'Royal Train' retained its LNWR livery and was only repainted in LMS maroon during the Second World War.   *P. S. Kendrick.*

LMS 0-6-0 No.**12053** on the Down Slow north of the station with a freight from Wichnor Junction to Stoke on Trent early in 1935. The engine was designed by Barton Wright for the Lancashire & Yorkshire Railway but at this time was shedded at Stoke on Trent. It has come from Wichnor Junction via Lichfield Upper and the spur to Lichfield Low Level, and at Colwich will take the North Staffordshire line to Stone. Normally this train would have taken the route via Burton and Uttoxeter but for some reason was diverted on this occasion. *P. S. Kendrick.*

Another heavy Down goods a little further north than the previous picture, in August 1937. The engine is Midland '3F' 0-6-0 No.**3709**, which was allocated to Burton shed for many years - its '17B' plate is on the smokebox door. It is heading for Salop Sidings, Stafford, where most of it will doubtless be reformed into a train for Swansea via Shrewsbury. Here, it is travelling on the Down Fast. In the remodelling for electrification the former fast and slow lines were interchanged north of Armitage, producing the inherently dangerous layout at Colwich which eventually resulted in the 1986 accident. This arrangement would never have been countenanced by the LNWR or LMS but still exists. *P. S. Kendrick.*

A Down express north of **Rugeley** in the early 1930s, hauled by 'Claughton' class 4-6-0 No.**5918** *Frederick Baynes*.   *P. S. Kendrick.*

An Up Trent Valley local at milepost 125, just north of **Rugeley**, hauled by a '19in Goods' class 4-6-0, about 1930.   *P. S. Kendrick.*

Another view of a Trent Valley local, taken at the same place as the lower picture opposite but in November 1949. By comparison, the train is now shorter and the engine is the first of the Nuneaton batch of Ivatt class '4' 2-6-0s, No.**43020**. This class was produced as a result of the LMS policy of building small modern engines for secondary workings instead of using large older engines displaced from the main line. Also gone are the tall signals, replaced by the colour lights in the extreme left of the picture, one of them positioned at ground level between the two Down tracks. *P. S. Kendrick.*

Another view at milepost 125, this time of a lengthy Up goods hauled by Stanier '8F' No.**8422** one evening in September 1947. Long mixed goods trains such as this were a common feature of the railway scene in the steam age and with their vast variety of loads provided a source of great fascination for enthusiasts. The colour light for the Down Slow can be seen on the extreme left, the fast line signal being between the tracks to the right. *P. S. Kendrick.*

Colwich

Fowler class '3P' 2-6-2 tank No.53 approaching the station on the Fast line with what appears to be a relief to a Down express in August 1935.
P. S. Kendrick.

'Rebuilt Royal Scot' No.**46158** *The Loyal Regiment* approaching the station with the Down 'Comet' on 6th September 1959. This Euston-Manchester express travelled via Stoke on Trent and the signal is 'off' for it to cross to the Stone line at the junction.
Edward Talbot.

Following 'The Comet' on 6th September 1959 was the Down 'Royal Scot'. Most unusually, instead of its booked 'Coronation' class Pacific, it was double-headed by 'Jubilee' No.**45686** *St. Vincent* and 'Rebuilt Scot' No.**46100** *Royal Scot* itself. The signal is 'off' for it to take the Stafford route.

Edward Talbot.

'Cauliflower' 0-6-0 No.**8524** leaving Colwich in August 1935 with what is thought to be a Stafford-Walsall local passenger train. The signals on the left control the junction north of Colwich station, the left-hand one being for the Stafford line, the right-hand one for Stone. *P. S. Kendrick.*

Colwich

Class '5' No.**44842**, recently ex works, passes on the Up Slow line on 6th September 1959. The train has come from Stafford and consists of empty mineral wagons - the rear of it is still on the junction.   *Edward Talbot.*

'Jubilee' class 4-6-0 No.**5563** accelerating away after slowing for the junction with an express from Manchester to Euston via Stoke about 1936. The engine was later named *Australia*.   *P. S. Kendrick*

'Jubilee' No.**5575**, later named *Madras*, passing the station with an early morning express from Euston to Manchester via Crewe in August 1935.
P. S. Kendrick.

North Staffordshire Railway 'New M' class 0-4-4 tank, LMS No.**1436**, awaiting the 'right away' with an early morning local passenger train from Walsall to Stoke on Trent in August 1935.   *P. S. Kendrick.*

Colwich

The exterior of Colwich station about 1950. The original Trent Valley building is on the left and the LNWR building on the right. *L.G.R.P. No.26739*

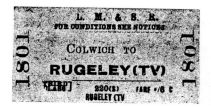

General view of Colwich station, looking north from the Up platform about 1900. *Bernard Matthews collection.*

View of Colwich station from the top of Colwich church tower. This is an excellent vantage point for the photographer but it is also a very dangerous one. The wall round the top of the tower is low, and the only place to stand, because of the shape of the roof, is a one-foot wide strip covered in very slippery pigeon droppings just inside it! *courtesy M. Burton.*

The Down 'Royal Scot' passing Colwich on 10th September 1959, hauled by 'Coronation' class Pacific No.**46242** *City of Glasgow*.

Edward Talbot.

Interior of the signal box in the 1950s.

David Bradbury

'Rebuilt Royal Scot' No.**46137** *The Prince of Wales Volunteers (South Lancashire)* bringing the 10am from Manchester to Euston via Stoke across the junction at Colwich. *Edward Talbot*

The same train as in the previous picture approaching Colwich station the following day behind type 4 diesel No. **D217**. *Edward Talbot*

An unidentified 'Rebuilt Claughton' approaching Colwich on the Stafford line with an Up express about 1932. *P. S. Kendrick*

Great Haywood

View of the North Staffordshire Railway station at Great Haywood about 1900. *courtesy S. Ball*

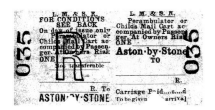

Sandon

(below).The mid-day Manchester-Euston express passing Sandon station hauled by 'Jubilee' class 4-6-0 No.**45644** *Howe* (20th April 1957). *Hugh B. Oliver.*

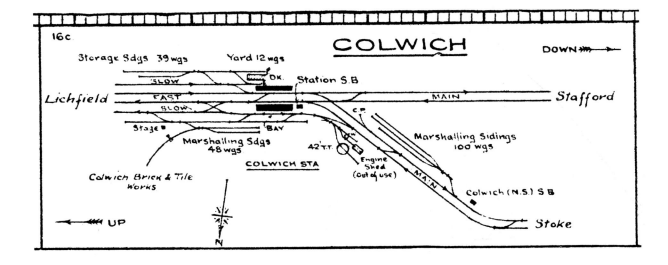

Stone

The London architect H.A. Hunt was perhaps better known for his work at Stoke on Trent station, but other North Staffordshire stations to his designs included Longport and Sandon as well as Stone, which, with its front elevation of three shaped or "Dutch" gables neatly fitted into the restricted site between the Norton Bridge and Colwich lines.

(above). View of the Colwich platforms at Stone, looking north about 1919.
Hugh B. Oliver.

(centre). This late 1950's view shows minimal change from that above although the flat canopy on the northbound platform has been removed. Regular train services to intermediate stations on the Stone to Colwich line ceased from 6th January 1947, although a morning return trip between Stone and Weston, and an evening northbound working from Colwich hardly deserves the term regular. The goods yard to the right saw public facilities withdrawn from 7th August 1967.

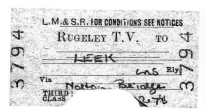

(below). The attractive outline of H.A. Hunt's design can be appreciated in this view of the station frontage taken across the Colwich lines. The junction is on the right, out of the picture, and the Norton Bridge lines are on the far side, behind the building. Platforms serving the Norton Bridge route have always been the busier of the four, a fact confirmed by the somewhat higher standard of passenger facility over the years.

Shugborough

'Patriot' class 4-6-0 No.**5996** leaving the south end of Shugborough tunnel with an Up express about 1935. This is the most northerly tunnel on the LNWR main line from Euston to Carlisle.
P. S. Kendrick.

Something of a rarity. The Southern Railway Sentinel railcar, built in 1933, approaching the south end of Shugborough tunnel. Presumably it is en route back to the Sentinel Works at Shrewsbury for repair. *P. S. Kendrick.*

The much admired 'Turbo', LMS No.**6202**, leaving Shugborough tunnel probably with the morning Liverpool-Euston express on 20th July 1937.
P. S. Kendrick.

LNWR 0-8-0 No.**49357** leaving Shugborough tunnel with an Up goods on 6th September 1959. The sign at the end of the tunnel reads 'Shugborough Tunnel, 777 yards'. *Edward Talbot.*

The Up 'Caledonian' leaving Shugborough tunnel on 10th September 1959, hauled by 'Coronation' class Pacific No.**46252** *City of Leicester.*
                                        Edward Talbot.

The north end of Shugborough tunnel as 'Royal Scot' No.**6144** *The Honourable Artillery Company* emerges with a Down express on 29th June 1935. It is only on summer evenings that the sun comes round sufficiently for pictures to be taken from this position.   *P. S. Kendrick.*

Milford & Brocton

'Coronation' class Pacific No. **46244** *King George VI* approaching Milford & Brocton with the Down 'Caledonian' on 18th August 1960. The woods in the background are in the grounds of Shugborough Hall, the home of Lord Lichfield, whose ancestor required the tunnel to be dug to preserve the views in the estate.   *Dr G. Smith.*

View from the east end of the overbridge at the south end of Milford & Brocton station, looking south west about 1910. The overbridge was built in 1877, when the station was opened, and replaced the level crossing, which passed roughly between the two signals. On the extreme right is the original crossing keeper's cottage, designed by Livock; it was demolished very quickly in December 1980. At this time, the four track section to Stafford began north of Milford station. The signal on the left controls the turn-out from the Down Main line into the Down Slow. The signal on the right controls the Up main line. There is a repeater signal at lower level (in shadow). The building in the centre background is a water company pumping station. It has now been demolished but the house beyond it still stands.

General view of Milford & Brocton station in the early 1950s, looking south towards Shugborough tunnel from the Down platform. The station name board is in the standard LMS colours of black letters on a yellow background.

LNWR 'Jumbo' 2-4-0 No.**193** *Rocket* and 'George the Fifth' 4-4-0 No.**1086** *Conway* north of Milford & Brocton with a Down express about 1920. At this time the fast lines were in the centre and the slow lines on either side; but this arrangement was changed when the line was electrified to conform with that north of Stafford, where the fast lines are on the Up side and the slow lines on the Down. *Roger Carpenter collection.*

'Patriot' class 4-6-0 No.**45520** *Llandudno* near Baswich, Stafford, with the Glasgow-Euston express which followed the 'Royal Scot'. In the distance on the left is the Vacuum Salt Works with its sidings off the main line. The works closed in the 1970s and the site is now used for mobile homes.
John B. Bucknall.

View of the crossing near Stafford, taken looking towards Stafford on the main Lichfield road, with the main line running from left to right across the picture about 1890. Queensville curve begins some 200 yards to the left. When the Trent Valley Railway was planned the mayor, burgesses and aldermen of Stafford presented the company with a petition. They claimed the road to Lichfield was sufficiently busy and important that a bridge should be built to carry it over the railway at this point. Nevertheless, Queensville Crossing was not replaced by a bridge until 28th June 1898, when the widening to four tracks of the main line between Stafford No.1 signal box at Trent Valley Junction and Milford & Brocton, came into use. The cabin and building on the left of the picture were then demolished.

Queensville

'Britannia' Pacific No. **70046** *Anzac* approaching Queensville signal box with an Up express in 1960 - the rear of the train is just coming off Queensville curve. When the tracks were rearranged in preparation for electrification, the Up Fast line became the Down Fast, and one of the signalmen recalls that he was often filled with horror as a northbound train sped past, his immediate reaction being that it was on the wrong track. A moment later, of course, he realised that everything was all right.

John B. Bucknall.

An unidentified LNWR 'Special DX' class 0-6-0 rounding Queensville curve past an old slotted signal in the early 1890s, probably with an Up Trent Valley local. At this time the line was still only double-track with a single up siding as far as Queensville. When the line was converted to four tracks, the additional tracks were added on the inside of the curve.

An Up goods setting off round Queensville curve, hauled by Stanier '8F' No.**48755** on 15th August 1960. Normally Stafford shed had no '8Fs' but this engine and one or two others were allocated to the shed for a short time when Hademore troughs were out of use. The LNWR 'Super Ds' had only 3000 gallon tenders and needed to rely on picking up water at Hademore. The '8Fs' with their larger tenders had a greater range. Stafford No.1 signal box controlling Trent Valley Junction is on the left. In the centre is a large brick building that was once a single-road engine shed, presumably for engines shunting in the south end yards. On top of it was a water tank which supplied the whole of the station area. Presumably at one time the water was treated in the tank but by this time a separate treatment plant was in use, the circular tower-like building to the right. Sludge from this plant was removed in old tenders. Behind the tank was Dinham's wagon repair shop. Three Manchester Ship Canal wagons, newly repaired and repainted, can be seen beyond the engine. *Edward Talbot.*

An Up express, probably a relief, heading up the Wolverhampton line at Trent Valley Junction c.1935, hauled by 'Experiment' class 4-6-0 No.25473 *Scottish Chief*. Partly hidden behind the train is a large ex-LNWR tank engine, possibly an 0-8-2 tank engaged on shunting in the yards.

P. S. Kendrick.

'Patriot' class 4-6-0 No. 45549 crossing Trent Valley Junction on the Down Slow line on 11th October 1960. The Grand Junction line to Wolverhampton goes off to the right. To the left of the shed and water tank are the workshops of W. E. Dinham & Sons, the wagon repair firm. Some more M. S. C. wagons are to the right of the shed. An engine is shunting on the Up siding and a Down express is signalled.

Edward Talbot.

View looking towards No. 4 signal box and Newport Road bridge on 14th January 1960. On the left is a 'Jinty' shunting a van and, nearest to the camera, an oil tank wagon lettered 'Walker's Century Oils'. During electrification No. 4 box was demolished and replaced by the present box sited against Newport Road bridge, roughly where the carriage is on the right of the picture.

General view looking north off Wolverhampton Road bridge, as 'Jubilee' class 4-6-0 No.**45631** *Tanganyika* leaves on an express for Wolverhampton and Birmingham in 1959. On the left are Salop Sidings; on the right are the south end sidings and No. 3 signal box.

John B. Bucknall.

The following photographs of wagons were taken in the yard at Stafford about 1910 to record instances of bad loading. Most of them might have had serious consequences but it is not known if any of them did. All are reproduced by courtesy of Staffordshire County Council Record Office.

(right). General view of a load of timber carried on two Cambrian Railways wagons, which had probably arrived in the yard off the Shrewsbury line.

(above). End view of the load of timber, showing how one log had shifted to a position where it might have struck another train or lineside fixture. On the left is the goods shed which still stands today.

(centre). View of the load of timber, taken from the other end looking north. Newport Road bridge is in the distance, while on the extreme right is No. 3 signal box. This box controlled the north end sidings on the up side and also access to a turntable situated just south of the bridge, to the right of the water column in the picture. Before the island platform was constructed on the down side at Stafford station in the early 1880s, this turntable was located north of Newport Road bridge on the Down side.

(lower). A load of planks that has partly tipped on to the next wagon, probably as a result of being shunted.

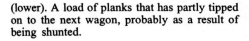

A wagon whose frame has been broken by the weight of a load of metal bars. Clearly, a longer flat wagon should have been used, in which the bars would not have been bent.

Another view of the 'broken' wagon, with Friars' Terrace in the background.

This wagon has been incorrectly sheeted; the sheet on the left has come adrift, allowing the sacks perhaps of grain or sugar to be exposed to rain.

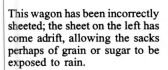

On 12th March 1906 the midnight express from Euston to Liverpool and Manchester was derailed while crossing from the Down Slow to Down Fast line at No. 4 box, just south of Newport Road bridge. Three carriages were wrecked when they collided with the bridge abutment and a brick building by it. The cause of the accident was never fully established but it was not due to excessive speed; the 20mph speed restriction was being observed at the time but nevertheless was later reduced to 10mph. This view of the general scene was taken the following morning, looking north from No. 4 box. The peculiarly shaped vehicle on the right is a tool van designed to work under the jib of a crane.

The 1906 Accident

View of the end of the brake van in the centre of the previous picture; it is West Coast Joint Stock brake van No.464, which was damaged beyond repair. On the right is Newport Road bridge with bridge number plate 84

View on the north side of Newport Road bridge, looking east from the Down side. The carriage, No.855, is a composite, with third class compartments at the outer ends and first in the centre. Behind it is the first LNWR steam breakdown crane, constructed on the orders of Mr Webb. Previously, the LNWR had used only hand cranes.

Another view of carriage No.855, taken from the other side.

The Station Front

Probably the earliest surviving photograph of the front of the station, taken about 1900. On the left is a horse-drawn cart, well loaded with baskets, and in the centre is a group of children, probably waiting to be picked up. On the right is the North Western Railway Hotel, while through the awning can be seen the pub well known to many generations of Stafford railwaymen, the Stafford Arms. *G.L. Turner collection.*

Another view of the front of the station, showing better detail of the entrance and awning, about 1910. There are two fine gas lamps on the wall to illuminate the entrance. In the distance, through the awning, can be seen the awning over the loading deck of the parcels office, which carts used to back up to. The spectators and two horse taxis have largely kept still for the benefit of the photographer and posterity.

courtesy Peter Rogers.

A smartly turned out horse trap belonging to W. H. Smith & Son posed outside the North Western Hotel (the word 'Railway' has now been removed) about 1914. No doubt it was used for collecting newspapers from the station and for delivery.

(left). View of the main street of Stafford about 1900 with an LNWR parcel van on the right. The Ancient High House on the right and the Bear Inn on the left fortunately still survive today.

(right). Emanuele Giusso, an Italian ice-cream maker and owner of a shop in Stafford, standing beside an LNWR dray loaded with blocks of ice in South Street with St Thomas's Church school in the background about 1910. The ice came from the Liverpool firm of T. Roope and was brought to Stafford by the LNWR. Orders telegraphed to the firm in the afternoon were delivered to most parts of the country the following morning.

Details of this picture are uncertain but it seems likely to have been taken to show a group of men, probably railwaymen, after enlisting in the armed forces at the beginning of the First World War. They are grouped on the pavement, to the right of the station canopy.

A view from the hotel balcony, possibly the visit of Edward Prince of Wales in 1928. The lean-to wooden building by the street lamp in the right background is the coffee tavern, which was used by railwaymen and other workers. Coffee taverns such as this were built at many LNWR stations and were owned by a limited company of which the railwaymen were shareholders. They provided refreshments of good quality at minimal cost. This one had a partition, so arranged that access was possible from the street and from the station but not from one to the other. The LNWR supported the company, partly perhaps because it kept the men out of its public refreshment rooms, which were more expensive anyway, and also out of the Stafford Arms. To the right of the coffee tavern are double gates giving access for parcel and postal traffic to the south end of platform 1. The other double gates further along the curved wall gave access to the bays at the south end of platform 1. They would have been used extensively in the days when horse-drawn carriages were conveyed by rail, to gain access to the loading ramps and bays.

View of the station front taken possibly at the same time as the previous picture. There appears to be bunting decorating the entrance under the awning. The hotel is now the 'Station Hotel'. On the extreme left, the sign reads: 'Dining and Tea Room Entrance on Platform'.

The station looking rather shabby in the late 1940s. Two gas lamps on the pavement, one of them leaning backwards, have replaced the elegant lamps previously on the wall and the 'Dining and Tea Room' notice has gone. This station of course had refreshment rooms and toilets on the Down as well as the Up side, in contrast to the modern station which has these facilities on the Up side only. The taxis belong to the firm of Adam's which served the station for many years.

Peter Rogers.

A view of the station front on 14th January 1960, a snowy January day, with the 'port-cochere' now removed.

Opposite (top). View of the station frontage from right of the entrance up to the parcels office loading deck on 29th February 1960. On the first floor of the building on the right was the BR Staff Association club with bar, snooker table and so forth.

Opposite (centre). The station frontage. Crewe can be reached for 3s 9d, Prestatyn for 13s, Rhyl for 13s 6d, Colwyn Bay for 15s and Llandudno for 16s 6d (17½p, 65p, 67½p, 75p and 82½p respectively). (29th February 1960).

Opposite (bottom). The station front with one of Adams' Rolls Royce taxis, platform barrows, bicycle leaning against wall (no doubt unlocked but safe from theft in those days) and snow-covered Jaguar saloon. (14th January 1960).

(top). A view of the main entrance but from a more acute angle on 14th January 1960.

(centre). View of the station front from left of the entrance up to the coffee tavern on 29th February 1960.

(lower). View from the coal yard looking towards Newport Road on 14th January 1960; the photographer is standing roughly where the car park of the present BR Staff Association club now is. The loaded lorry on the right is heading for Newport Road with the Grammar School cricket pitch on its right. At the road junction it will either turn right into town or left and then either over Newport Road bridge or round past the front of the station.

all views: British Rail L.M. Region.

View looking along Railway Street towards the station on 29th February 1960. On the right is the roof over the Great Northern bays and north end of platform 1. Then comes the parcels office with lorries outside waiting to be unloaded. On the left is the inn sign for the 'Stafford Arms' (Butler's Ales) and below it another sign 'Booking Office, Happy Days' (Austin's buses and coaches).

The parcels office with a van being unloaded on 14th January 1960. On the right is part of the Station Hotel and some houses, then the Stafford Arms and on the corner of Derby Street Austin's booking office. The road is covered with slush from melting snow.

The Platforms

View looking along the main Up platform, platform 1, about 1900, with station staff lined up at a suitable distance from the camera. The crowd beyond has perhaps come from the train in the Great Northern bay at the far end of the platform. There is a Down train in platform 2 and a light engine on the Down Through line.

Brookside Photographic .

Another view from about the same period, again looking north along platform 1 but from a little further to the south. Clearly the 11.15am to Euston is expected. The adjustable clock on the right, with its finger boards for the various destinations, was a common feature of many LNWR stations and lasted well into the early BR period.

Brookside Photographic.

View looking across from platform 2 to platform 1 as an Up express approaches from the left. The notice reads 'Passengers and Others Must Cross the Line by the Overbridge'.

View looking north along platform 4 (2 in LNWR and LMS days). In the left foreground is an enamel sign in BR maroon and white. Signs like this replaced the old large wooden signs which in LMS days had black letters on a yellow background. *H. C. Casserley*.

The Railway Magazine Article, July 1907
In its early years *The Railway Magazine* had a series on 'Notable Stations' and the July 1907 issue covered Stafford. These illustrations are taken from that issue and though of poor quality due to being copied from the magazine show features not to be found in other pictures.

View of Trent Valley Junction from Wolverhampton Road bridge. On the left is a Webb three-cylinder compound heading south along the Up main line, while a Down train approaches on the right. It is probably a goods as it is signalled on to the slow line. On the Trent Valley line the fast lines are in the centre. The slow lines are on either side of them with connections to the Down side yard. Again, comparison with the layout in later pictures is rewarding.

Broadside view of the front of the station.

A local train to Shrewsbury leaving bay 4, hauled by a 'Teutonic' three-cylinder compound. This class worked from Shrewsbury after being displaced from the main line.

The north end of Stafford station as seen by the signalman in No. 5 box. The tracks are, from left to right: the Great Northern bays; platform 1; the through lines; platform 2; bay 4, with a North Stafford train awaiting departure to the Potteries; platform 3; the slow lines round the back of the station; and the line for engines leaving or going on the shed. The train on the Down Slow is signalled to take the Shrewsbury line. The track layout shown in this picture is worth comparing with those which follow. In general the trend was towards making the layout more simple.

(above). The station master, Mr Cooke, posing for the camera on platform 3. This platform was used by local trains to and from Birmingham, Nuneaton, Shrewsbury and Stoke on Trent. Thanks to the scissors crossing, two trains could be at the platform and either one could leave in either direction without being blocked by the other.

(right-centre). The north end of the station with an unidentified 'Precursor' approaching on the Down Through line and North Stafford tank No.18 waiting to leave on a local service to Stoke on Trent.

View looking south towards Bagnall's bridge, taken from the signal gantry spanning the four-track section north of the junction with the Great Northern branch on the left and the Shrewsbury line on the right. The siding on this side of the GN line serves Venables' timber yard (the firm was founded in 1864); beyond the branch is Hall's coal yard, which was served off the branch itself. On the right is the Castle Works of W. G. Bagnall, founded in 1876, while beyond the bridge is No. 5 signal box and the signal gantry which was only a matter of feet from the bridge.

The Floods of 1946

Torrential rain on Friday 8th February 1946 caused extensive flooding in Stafford with the result that train services had to be suspended in the early hours of 9th February. Road services were provided for passengers to Penkridge, Norton Bridge, Newport and Colwich and main-line services were diverted. The main line to Crewe was also blocked by a landslide at Wrinehill. Rail services were restored shortly after 2pm on Sunday 10th February. Northwards to Crewe the slow lines were re-opened on Monday and the fast lines on Thursday, thousands of tons of ballast being used in making good the slip. Fortunately the well known Stafford photographer Peter Rogers, who founded the business which still trades in Mill Street today, took extensive photographs of the floods, including a number of the station. The pictures which follow were all taken by him. Further flooding occurred in Stafford the following March when the heavy snow and frosts of that exceptionally severe winter finally thawed, but train services were not affected. Much work has been done subsequently by the river authorities to enable flood water to be carried away quickly. A sad consequence has been that in normal times the river through the town is a mere trickle but at least the work has been successful in putting an end to flooding.

View along Station Road to Newport Road. Only two buildings in this picture are still standing, the Eagle Inn (largely hidden by the houses in the right foreground) and the building next to it.

The north end of the station looking south off Bagnall's bridge. The water draws attention to the wooden walkways provided for the cleaners working on carriages in the sidings on the left.

Two views of the south end of the station looking northwards off Newport Road bridge with sundry pieces of timber floating about. The way in which the south end of platform 1 narrowed to allow space for a siding alongside the platform line can be clearly seen.

Inside the station, looking north along platform 2. The hand-worked point lever presumably operated the points to enable a train to set back into the sidings leading back to the bridge abutment or to the Up Slow line.

Two porters pose appropriately with a box of fish from Fleetwood!

The scene at Doxey Road coal depot looking from Broad Eye bridge away from the town, an area which was always amongst the first to be flooded. This depot was served off the Great Northern branch.

Throughout the LMS period and until the early 1950s the station remained essentially as it was in the late years of the LNWR but then alterations began to be made, as can be seen by comparison with the lower picture on this page and elsewhere. The most obvious alteration was the gradual replacement of the standard LNWR signals and signal gantries with colour lights and steel gantries; the removal of 'Big Ben', the tall signal on the up fast line, was greatly lamented by enthusiasts (but not, no doubt, by the man who had had to climb it in the days of oil lamps!). Other alterations were the removal of the sidings between the Down platform and Newport Road bridge, enabling the platform to be extended slightly, and the partial cutting back of the overall roof at the south end of platform 1 and erection of the structures seen here. The need for this may have been damage caused by a fire under the roof in May 1955, when the fire brigade had to be called. On the extreme left is an unusual signal with four arms vertically above one another. It controls engines coming off the shed along the Down Slow and proceeding in the Up direction; from top to bottom the arms lead to the yard on the Up side, the Up Fast, the Up Slow and Salop sidings.   *John B. Bucknall.*

General view of the south end of Stafford station taken from Newport Road bridge about 1925. This picture emphasises the fact that the various bays and sidings were extensively used for parcels and other traffic.   *S. H. P. Higgins*

Something of a mystery picture in that the carriage carries the nameboard of the Merseyside Express, a train which was not normally scheduled to stop at Stafford. However, there was a Liverpool to Birmingham working at this time, which attached additional carriages from Manchester at Crewe, hence the length of the train. This view looking along platform 6 was taken in 1956.

G.H. Platt.

In LNWR days both bays at the south end of platform 1 were used for local passenger trains but by the late 1940s only bay 2 was so used. Here about 1905 Webb '5ft 6in 2-4-2 Tank' No.**133** stands in bay 1 awaiting departure with a local train, probably for the Trent Valley line. It is a Stafford engine, its '14' shed plate being in the usual position on the back of the cab roof. Through the bridge on the right can be seen No.4 signal box and the fine signal gantry beside it, while the gantry controlling exit from the bays is largely hidden behind the engine.

A. E. L. Thorne, courtesy V. R. Webster.

(opposite). Bracket signal controlling exit from the bays at the south end of platform 1. The building behind it is believed to have originally been the lamp room, where all the oil lamps in the station, signals and surrounding area where cleaned and refilled by the lamp porters. Lamp rooms were generally sited some distance from stations because of the risk of fire from the store of oil. In the 1950s the building housed the carriage and wagon department and also some offices of the signal and telegraph department. The main offices of the latter were on the other side of Newport Road bridge on the Down side in a building which still stands today. On the left are railway houses which survived until the rebuilding of the station.   *E. S. Russell.*

(below). View looking across to the south end of platform 1 from platform 2. On the left 'Jumbo' No.**868** *Condor* waits to depart from platform 1. To the right of it '5ft 6in 2-4-2 Tank' No.**133** stands in the bay, while in the siding is LNWR carriage truck No.586.

      R. S. Carpenter collection.

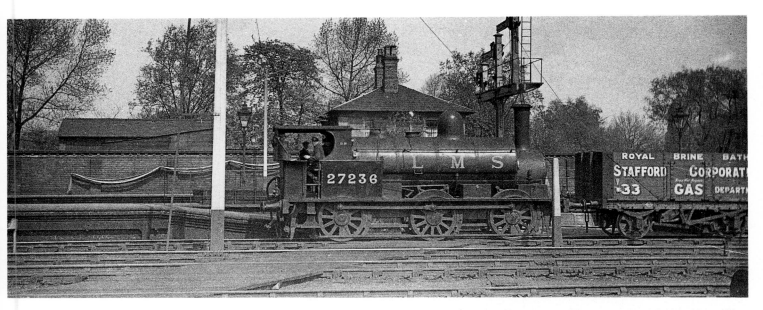

Ramsbottom 'Special Tank' No.27236 at the south end of platform 1. It is propelling its train into the sidings south of Newport Road bridge (the 'calling on' signal on the gantry above the engine is 'off'); the other two signals control exit from the platform to the Up Slow line and to the Up Fast line. The wagon belonging to the Stafford Corporation Gas Department is believed to have been painted a bright red colour. Above the engine can be seen the roof of the station master's house. During electrification the station master was rehoused, and this building was used for the BR Staff Association club after the station was demolished and until the new one was built near the coal wharf.
P. S. Kendrick..

The same engine poses for the photographer while shunting vans in the bay at the south end of the down platform in 1935. 'Big Ben' disappears out of sight on the right!
P. S. Kendrick.

Stanier class '3P' 2-6-2 tank No.**40122** in the same bay but photographed from the south end of platform 1. Stafford did not normally have any engines of this class but it was on loan for a time in 1959 and was used as station pilot. The postal sorting office is in the background on the left.   *Edward Talbot.*

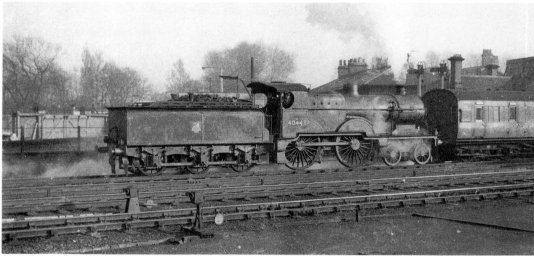

In the 1940s and 1950s the Stafford station pilot was invariably an ex-Midland '2P' 4-4-0, LMS Nos. **443** and **461** usually being employed on the job. In LNWR days it had been the practice to employ engines capable of assisting main-line expresses if required but it is doubtful whether either of these two venerable machines was ever required to perform in this way. Here, on a winter's day in 1957 driver Jack Ecclestone with No.**40443** propels some vans along the down slow line out of platform 1.   *Edward Talbot.*

The most glamorous train put on by the LMS was 'The Coronation Scot', which provided a service between London and Glasgow in 6½ hours. Special streamlined engines and coaches were built for it, painted in a striking livery of blue with silver stripes. Here, 'Coronation' class 4-6-2 No.**6221** *Queen Elizabeth* passes under Newport Road bridge and approaches the station with the northbound service in April 1938. Track remodelling was carried out at several points, including the Queensville curve and Trent Valley Junction, to enable high speeds to be maintained.   *E. S. Russell.*

'Rebuilt Royal Scot' No.**46140** *The King's Royal Rifle Corps* rolls into Stafford with an express from London to Blackpool in 1958. By comparison with the previous picture there are no sidings on the right and the platform has been extended slightly. *Edward Talbot.*

The first of the 'Jubilees' No.**45552** *Silver Jubilee* at the same spot but on the through line with an express from Birmingham to Liverpool in the summer of 1958.   *Edward Talbot.*

In the 1950s BR put on a high-speed service between Euston and Glasgow like 'The Coronation Scot' but without streamlined engines and stock, and called it 'The Caledonian'. Here, in 1959, the up train passes through the station hauled by 'Coronation' class Pacific No.**46228** *Duchess of Rutland.*
Edward Talbot.

Normally the 'Royal Scot' passed through Stafford non-stop in both directions but even in the best regulated organisations and with the best engines, things occasionally go wrong. One day in the summer of 1956 Stanier Pacific No.46253 *City of St. Albans* 'dropped a plug' on the approach to Stafford; both injectors had failed, perhaps caused by dirt in the water, and the water level in the boiler fell to the extent that one of the fusible plugs began to melt, forcing the driver to fail the engine at Stafford. The only engine on the shed in reasonable order to take its place was class '5' No.45250. It is seen here restarting the train from platform 1.

Edward Talbot.

The water column at the south end of platform 1 on 22nd March 1957. It is of standard LNWR design and is located between the platform line and Up main line so as to serve both. Upside down on the right are two fire braziers which would be put to good use in winter preventing the column and the bag from freezing up.   *E. S. Russell.*

In the 1940s and 1950s there were at least two trips a day from the north end yard on the Up side south of the station to Stafford Common with traffic for the gas works, salt works and RAF 16 MU. These trips were invariably worked by '3F' 0-6-0 tanks, often referred to as 'Jinties' by enthusiasts but as 'Humpies' (an old LNWR term for a shunting engine) by Stafford enginemen. Here, long-time Stafford engine No.47588 passes through platform 1 with a return working to the yard.   *Edward Talbot.*

'Coronation' class Pacific No.**46256** *Sir William A. Stanier F. R. S.* waiting for the 'right away' from platform 1 with an Up express on 2nd August 1958. It is well off the platform, having drawn up its 17-coach load to allow access to the rear vehicles from the platform. 'Drawing up' was commonplace in the 1940s and early 1950s at both up and down platforms, since loads of 15, 16 and 17 coaches were normal on many services, particularly on Liverpool trains, and neither platform could accommodate so many.   *J. B. Bucknall.*

General view of the south end of the station in 1958. An Up express stands in platform 1 headed by a 'Rebuilt Royal Scot' and another express is in the Down platform. On the left of the picture, trains are signalled on both Up and Down Slow lines, and the track layout at the back of the station can be clearly seen, the scissors crossing, No. 6 signal box and so forth, and in the distance the coaling plant at the shed.   *Edward Talbot.*

LNWR 'Problem' class 2-2-2 No.**279** *Stephenson* waiting by No. 6 signal box to back off the shed to collect its train, possibly a local to Shrewsbury, about 1905. Stafford shed had an allocation of these engines for very many years and was one of the last sheds to have them up to withdrawal in 1907. Among the advertisements on the hoarding behind the engine is one for Brookfields, the well known local outfitters; the name forms each of the four sides of the diamond shapes in the advertisement.
R. S. Carpenter collection.

Webb 'Cauliflower' 0-6-0 No.**2466** standing on the Up Slow line by No.6 box about 1905. It appears to be attached to the rear of a permanent way train, as the brake van has the word 'ballast' on its number plate.
R. S. Carpenter collection.

Another 'Cauliflower', LMS No.**8597** of shed '9', Walsall, on the slow line by No. 6 box about 1935 with an empty stock train. Even when other sheds had lost their LNWR 0-6-0s in the late 1940s and early 1950s, those allocated to Nuneaton, both '17in Coal Engines' and '18in Goods' or 'Cauliflowers', worked to Stafford regularly on the morning pick up goods from Nuneaton, arriving in Stafford around midday.
P. S. Kendrick.

An Up Liverpool-London express, hauled by 'Princess Royal' 4-6-2 No.**46211** *Queen Maud* standing in platform 6 one Sunday morning in 1959. Normally this platform was used for local passenger and parcel trains only. It was extremely rare for it to be occupied by an express passenger train and even rarer by one travelling in the Up direction. On this occasion, however, platform 1 was out of use due to permanent way work. *Edward Talbot.*

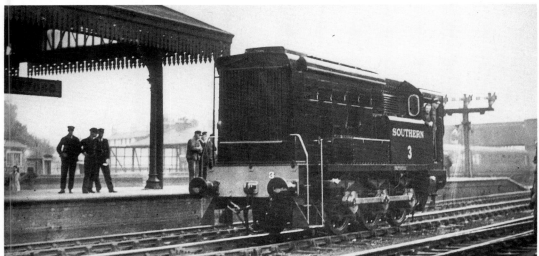

In steam days it was not unusual for light engines to pass through Stafford en route to and from the various works. For example, engines from LNWR classes such as 0-8-2 and 0-8-4 tanks, not in everyday use at Stafford, were occasionally seen on their way to and from Rugby Works, and similarly engines shedded in South Wales were sometimes seen on their way to Derby. Most common among the latter were '3F' 0-6-0 tanks but on one memorable day in 1946 '1P' 2-4-0 LMS No.**20155** appeared. However unusual all these were, this must have caused a sensation - the third Southern Railway diesel-electric shunter being delivered to the Southern in September 1937.

F. W. Shuttleworth collection

Fowler 2-6-4 tank engines were stationed at Stafford for many years for working local passenger trains to Birmingham, Manchester via Stoke, Wellington and Shrewsbury, and also for certain goods turns. Here No.**42389** has just come off the shed and waits to cross over to the south end sidings (on the Up side) for a pick up goods turn. It will take any traffic for Penkridge and empties for Littleton Colliery, and return from there with coal traffic and wagons from the goods station to the south end sidings. It will then take any traffic for Great Bridgeford, Norton Bridge and Badnall Wharf, including gunpowder empties and fulls, and return with traffic from the same stations including munitions from the factory at Swynnerton into the south end sidings. Stafford had this job and used a 2-6-4 tank on it regularly until the munitions factory closed in 1956, shortly after this photograph was taken. *Edward Talbot.*

'Prince of Wales' No.**25689** *Caliban* standing in platform 3, probably with a Shrewsbury local, in the late 1930s.

From time to time engines for which there was temporarily no work were put into store, which in practice meant putting them in a siding after covering the chimney to prevent rain getting into the smokebox and cylinders, and greasing the motion. One siding used occasionally for this purpose was that by No. 6 box, which is to the left of this picture. Here it accommodates Midland '2P' 4-4-0 No.**40332**.

F. W. Shuttleworth.

Burton engines regularly worked to Stafford via Wichnor Junction and Lichfield, mostly with traffic to South Wales via Shrewsbury, and Stafford engines of course worked to Burton. Here, '4F' 0-6-0 No.**44541**, complete with Burton shed plate '17B', waits to move off the shed and proceed to the goods yard to collect its train on 12th August 1960. No.6 box is on the right. In the distance, between the box and the engine tender, can be seen the 'lodge' attached to Stafford shed. This was built by the LNWR to accommodate enginemen from other sheds who worked into Stafford, booked off, went to the lodge to eat and sleep, and then booked on again to work back to their home sheds. Mostly these sheds were some distance from Stafford but some were quite near. It seems unbelievable nowadays but Crewe South had a lodging turn to Stafford in the 1930s, with the daily pick up goods which left Crewe at 9.20am and shunted 'every gatepost' to Stafford. The men returned with the corresponding working from Stafford the following day. This lodging turn probably dated back well into LNWR days. During the war it was changed so that crews from either end changed over half way. The pick up goods trains between Walsall and Stafford via Rugeley Trent Valley were also worked as lodging turns at the same period, by Walsall men. These lodging turns had ceased by the late 1940s but the lodge was still used by shed staff such as the 'lads from Wales', young men who had moved from South Wales to Stafford to work as cleaners and firemen, and had no home of their own in the town. It was closed in 1961 and later demolished but the shed of course still stands, having been converted to industrial use in 1989.

Edward Talbot.

In the bay on the right are '3F' 0-6-0 tank No.**47475** and an Ivatt class '2' tender engine 2-6-0 on an inspection saloon.

Three views of platform 6 all taken from roughly the same position near No. 6 signal box on 29th February 1960.

Platform 6 was on the Down side at Stafford, overlooking the slow lines. The platform road was bi-directional with the scissors crossover, so typical of former LNWR stations, giving much operational flexibility.

The north end of the platform with a diesel multiple unit in the bay awaiting departure for Manchester via Stoke.

The first engine shed at Stafford was brought into use early in 1838 by the Grand Junction Railway to house a spare engine but little is known of it. This is the earliest known photograph of Stafford shed, taken from platform 3 in the late 1890s. On the right is No.1 shed, erected for the Northern Division; on the left is No.2 shed, erected for the Southern Division in the 1860s. The engine on the left is Webb experiment compound No.**302** *Velocipede*; the other engines include a 'Problem' 2-2-2, a 'Special DX', a '17in Coal Engine' and a 'Cauliflower'. At this time along the whole of the inside of one wall of the shed were stacks of wooden brake blocks of different shapes and sizes to suit the various classes; men were employed for the sole purpose of cutting new ones. This went on until after the First World War.   *D. J. Patrick collection.*

A poor photograph but one which shows the layout of the shed in the late LNWR and early LMS period. No.2 shed is on the left and No.1 on the right. Alongside No.1 shed is the road used by coal wagons on their way to the 'coal hole'. Engines to be coaled ran alongside the 'coal hole' and further along the same track was the turntable. After turning, engines came back 'shed side', that is, alongside No.2 shed.

LNWR 'Precursor' class 4-4-0 No.**2164** *Oberon* at Stafford shed about 1905. The engines on the right are waiting to be coaled at the 'coal hole' alongside No.1 shed. To the left is No.2 shed.
        R. S. Carpenter collection.

During the First World War lady cleaners were employed at the shed in place of men who had been recruited into the armed forces. Here, in the shed yard a group of them pose for the camera with the shed foreman, T. L. P. ('Tommy') Howard on the left and the foreman cleaner. The engine is 'Experiment' class No.**1420** *Derbyshire*. It is facing south and seems to have been specially cleaned, perhaps for working an excursion or ambulance train

The 'Renown' class 4-4-0 *Good Hope* outside No. 2 shed in the early 1920s. It has no visible number, having lost its LNWR number plate, but was LMS No.**5127**. On the right is a 'Super D'. *Ken Wood collection*.

Engines at Stafford Shed

Engine sheds were officially described on the LNWR as 'locomotive steam sheds' and were numbered in a list from 1 to 38. Stafford was shed 14. Each engine displayed the number of the shed it was allocated to on an oval enamel plate which clipped into a bracket on the rear edge of the cab roof. The plate had black figures on a white background.

In early LMS days the LNWR numbers continued at first except that after a while the plates were displayed on smokebox doors. New codes covering all the sheds on the LMS were introduced in 1935, and Stafford then became shed 5C, under Crewe North, shed 5A. Cast-iron shed plates were used, fitted to the smokebox doors. Stafford continued as shed 5C throughout the LMS and early BR era until closure in 1965.

The following lists show engines allocated to Stafford shed at various dates. Under the LNWR engines did not stay at one shed for a long time. When an engine went to Crewe Works for overhaul, it was replaced by a newly overhauled engine of the same class and after overhaul was sent to the first shed needing an engine of that class. In LMS days engines usually returned to their home sheds after overhaul but were still transferred from one shed to another quite often.

1855 (Northern Division)
6ft 'Crewe Single' 2-2-2: **33** *Erebus*, **34** *Phoebus*, **37** *Hawk*, **43** *Vampire*, **44** *Harlequin*, **54** *Medusa*, **109** *Queen*, **111** *Russell*, **167** *Rhinoceros*, **184** *Problem*, **188** *Colonel*, **192** *Hero*, **199** *Castor*, **224** *Violet*. 5ft 'Crewe Goods' 2-4-0: **133** *Ostrich*, **254** *Theseus*, **312** *Tubal*, **328** *Czar*, **336** *Woodcock*, **360** *Theodore*.

1877 (part list)
'Problem' 2-2-2: **1** *Saracen*, **7** *Scorpion*, **44** *Harlequin*, **117** *Tiger*, **134** *Owl*, **139** *Cygnet*, **165** *Star*, **218** *Wellington*, **222** *Lily*, **229** *Watt*, **230** *Monarch*, **234** *Mazeppa*, **279** *Stephenson*, **291** *Prince of Wales*, **719** *Outram*, **754** *Ethelred*, **762** *Locke*, **804** *Soult*, **827** *Victoria*, **1435** *Fortuna*, **1436** *Egeria*. 'Samson' 2-4-0: **746** *Castor*, **828** *Tubal*, **830** *Trent*, **885** *Vampire*, **934** *North Star*, **1045** *Whitworth*. 'DX' 0-6-0: **1163**. 5ft 'Crewe Goods' 2-4-0: **1852** *Jason*, **1880** *Chandos*, **1899** *Raven*, **1918** *Goldfinch*. Sharp 2-2-2 Tank: **631**.

1911
'Jubilee' 4-6-0: **1904** *Rob Roy*, **1905** *Black Diamond*. 'Large Jumbo' 2-4-0: **304** *Hector*, **865** *Envoy*, **1668** *Dagmar*. 'Small Jumbo' 2-4-0: **231** *Firefly*, **479** *Mastodon*. 'Superheater 4-6-2 Tank': **376**, **1638**. '5ft 6in 2-4-2 Tank': **133**, **960**, **1148**, **1383**, **1766**. 'Bill Bailey': **545**, **1429**. 'Cauliflower' 0-6-0: **332**, **348**, **464**, **471**, **755**, **1028**, **1221**, **1244**, **1780**, **2208**. 'Special DX' **3008**, **3135**, **3295**, **3385**, **3428**. 'G1' 0-8-0: **2349**. 'D' 0-8-0: **1873**. 'Coal Tank': **443**. 'Special Tank': **707**, **880**, **3226**, **3542**. 'Bissell Tank': **3469**.

1917
'Experiment' 4-6-0: **828** *City of Liverpool*, 'Precursor' 4-4-0: **561** *Antaeus*, **639** *Ajax*, **1396** *Harpy*. 'Renown' 4-4-0: **1936** *Royal Sovereign*, 'Benbow' 4-4-0: **1944** *Victoria and Albert*, **1958** *Royal Oak*, **1973** *Hood*. 'Jubilee' 4-4-0: **1916** *Irresistible*: 'Large Jumbo' 2-4-0: **477** *Caractacus*, **945** *Humphrey Davy*. 'Small Jumbo' 2-4-0: **1045** *Whitworth*, **1522** *Pitt*, **1682** *Novelty*. 'Superheater 4-6-2 Tank': **2665**. '5ft 6in 2-4-2 Tank': **1398**, **1760**, **2134**. '19in Goods'

4-6-0: **1782**. 'Cauliflower' 0-6-0: **600**, **914**, **1267**, **1771**. 'SDX' 0-6-0: **3128**, **3149**, **3359**, **3441**. 'G1' 0-8-0: **1127**, **1790**. 'Special Tank' 0-6-0ST: **1129**, **3218**, **3298**, **3307**. 'Bissell Tank': **3525**.

1920
'Experiment' 4-6-0: **1406** *George Findlay*, **1420** *Derbyshire*, **1703** *Northumberland*, **1709** *Princess May*, **2628** *Banshee*. 'George the Fifth' 4-4-0: **752** *John Hick*, **1532** *Bloodhound*. 'Precursor' 4-4-0: **510** *Albatross*, **837** *Friar*, **1509** *America*, **2585** *Watt*. 'Benbow' 4-4-0: **1941** *Alfred the Great*, **1958** *Royal Oak*, **1962** *Aurora*, **1964** *Caesar*, **1970** *Good Hope*. 'Large Jumbo' 2-4-0: **480** *Duchess of Lancaster*, **787** *Clarendon*, **857** *Prince Leopold*, **1745** *Glow-worm*, **2185** *Alma*, **2187** *Penrith Beacon*. 'Small Jumbo' 2-4-0: **486** *Skiddaw*. '5ft 6in 2-4-2 Tank': **1378**, **1451**. '19in Goods' 4-6-0: **992**, **1058**, **1450**, **1538**, **1786**, **2588**. 'Cauliflower' 0-6-0: **349**, **450**, **534**, **1139**, **1502**, **1719**, **1740**. 'Special DX' 0-6-0: **3002**, **3128**. 'C1' 0-8-0: **1875**. 'Piano G' 0-8-0: **1887**, **1900**. 'G1' 0-8-0: **1167**, **2199**. 'Special Tank' 0-6-0ST: **3052**, **3182**, **3211**, **3298**, **3663**.

1933
'Precursor': **5199** *Cedric*, **5230** *Arab*, **5275** *Tiger*, 'Rebuilt Precursor': **5274** *Hecate*, **5276** *Titan*, **5277** *Oberon*, **5278** *Precursor*, **5279** *Sunbeam*, **5280** *Shooting Star*, **5281** *Erebus*. 'Prince of Wales': **5602** *Bonaventure*, **5667** *Zamiel*, **5689** *Caliban*, **5825**, **5826**, **5827**, **5830**. 'Superheater 4-6-2 Tank': **6989**, **6991**, **6992**. 'Special Tank' 0-6-0ST: **7420**. 'Cauliflower' 0-6-0: **8516**, **8523**, **8524**, **8525**. '19in Goods 4-6-0: **8735**, **8766**, **8767**, **8784**, **8798**, **8801**, **8855**. Ex-LNWR '7F' 0-8-0: **9019**, **9021**, **9022**, **9239**. Fowler class '3P' 2-6-2 Tank: **15550**, **15551**. Class '3F' 0-6-0 Tank: **16681**, **16682**, **16683**.

1945
Midland class '2P' 4-4-0: **443**, **461**. Stanier class '4' 2-6-4 Tank: **2537**, **2565**, **2614**. Class '3F' 0-6-0 Tank: **7294**, **7588**, **7598**, **7606**, **7649**, **7670**. Ex-LNWR '7F' 0-8-0: **8940**, **9031**, **9091**, **9098**, **9113**, **9144**, **9194**, **9320**. 'Prince of Wales' 4-6-0: **25648** *Queen of the Belgians*, **25674** *Scott*, **25725**, **25749**, **25775**, **25787**, **25841**. 'Cauliflower' 0-6-0: **28592**.

1950
Midland class '2P' 4-4-0: **40322**, **40405**, **40443**, **40461**, **40471**, **40507**. Fowler class '4' 2-6-4 Tank: **42320**, **42345**, **42346**, **42347**, **42391**. Class '3F' 0-6-0 Tank: **47588**, **47598**, **47606**, **47649**, **47653**, **47665**. Ex-LNWR '7F' 0-8-0: **48922**, **49047**, **49115**, **49158**, **49229**, **49410**.

1959
LMS class '2P' 4-4-0: **40583**, **40646**, **40678**. Class '4' 2-6-4 Tank: **42309**,

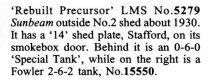

North Staffordshire Railway 0-6-4 tank engine, LMS No.**2055**, outside the shed in the late 1920s. On the left is an LNWR superheated 0-8-0 and on the right an '18in' 0-6-2 tank.

'Rebuilt Precursor' LMS No.**5279** *Sunbeam* outside No.2 shed about 1930. It has a '14' shed plate, Stafford, on its smokebox door. Behind it is an 0-6-0 'Special Tank', while on the right is a Fowler 2-6-2 tank, No.**15550**.

View of the shed taken from the north end of platform 3 through the gantry over the slow lines about 1936. The shed is crowded with engines of many types. On the far left is an LMS 'Jubilee' as yet un-named. Next to it is an LNWR superheated passenger engine, a 'Precursor' or a 'Prince'. Then comes an LMS compound 4-4-0 and a Stanier 2-6-2 tank, both facing into the shed. Next is a line of engines waiting to be coaled or reach the turntable: 'Cauliflower' 0-6-0 No.**8561**, an unidentified 'Super D' and an LMS 'Crab' 2-6-0. On the right is the 'coal hole', with wagons of coal outside waiting to be pushed up the ramp and unloaded. All in all, a very busy scene typical of the railways in steam days.

'Cauliflower' 0-6-0 No. **8524** with '5C' Stafford shed plate, standing by the 'coal hole' about 1936. Coaling was done by labourers who filled small tubs with coal either directly from wagons or off the floor where it had been shovelled out. A full tub was then pushed against a kind of metal flap, which was pivoted at its base. The flap then dropped to the horizontal position and the tub was pushed out on to it and tipped into the tender below. In this picture the flap is in the raised position above the engine cab. When there was a queue of engines waiting for the 'coal hole', some engines were coaled directly from coal wagons in sidings at the west side of the shed. This was very hard work for the labourers, who had to shovel the coal up and over the side of the wagon into the engine tender, though once the floor of the wagon had been reached it became easier. In the early 1920s these men were paid a 'tanner a day and a tanner a ton' (a 'tanner', 6d, was the equivalent of 2½p).   *R. S. Carpenter collection.*

In the late 1930s the LMS initiated a programme of shed modernisation to reduce costs and improve efficiency by organising servicing in a rational way. When an engine arrived at a shed, it first took water and coal, next it passed to the ash plant for the fire to be cleaned and then it continued to the turntable to be turned if necessary. Finally it went to the shed for any repairs to be carried out before the next turn of duty. This view shows the coaling plant built at Stafford. Coal wagons were hoisted on a platform to be tipped bodily into a hopper from which it was fed to the engine. This enormous structure weighed over 800 tons and is reputed to have caused three contractors attempting to build it to go bankrupt, as they failed to calculate the cost of the foundations in the marshy Stafford ground. Here, a 'Prince of Wales' 4-6-0 is being coaled, while a '17in Coal Engine' is on the ash plant, which was also of concrete but much smaller. Ashes from the firebox and smokebox were dropped between the rails into a pit, from where they were hoisted into a hopper by a bucket. From time to time an empty wagon was run beneath the hopper and the ashes dropped into it. This was a great advance on LNWR days when ashes were dropped anywhere in the yard and cleared away by labourers with barrows. When the new coal and ash plants were brought into use, No. 1 shed and the old LNWR 'coal hole' were demolished. The new arrangements were a great improvement and did away with much hard physical labour. No doubt the services of many labourers were no longer needed.

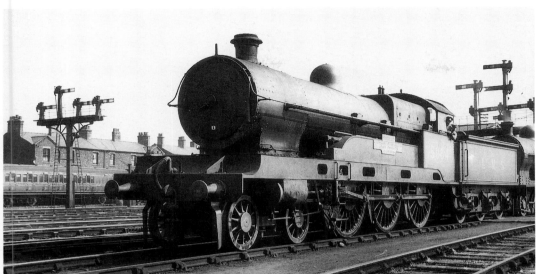

A famous visitor to Stafford shed, 'Claughton' No.**5964** *Patriot*, taken about 1931. This was the LNWR war memorial engine and was so named in honour and remembrance of the employees of the company who lost their lives in the First World War. It has a Rugby shed plate, '8'.

A distinguished visitor. 'Royal Scot' No.**6106** *Gordon Highlander* outside the shed about 1940, with two LMS compounds on the left. Large engines such as 'Scots' visited the shed occasionally, and Stanier 'Jubilees', class '5s' and '8F' 2-8-0s regularly, but no large engines were allocated to Stafford until near the end of steam when one or two class '5s' and '8Fs' arrived.

'Rebuilt Precursor' No.**25277** on the shed about 1945 with the coaling plant behind it to the left. This picture makes a striking contrast with the earlier view of the same engine (page 72 - bottom). The world had changed enormously in the forty years from 1905, as it has again in the forty five years since this picture was taken. *R. S. Carpenter collection.*

Stafford was the last shed to be home to the former LNWR 'Prince of Wales' class 4-6-0s. Though originally main-line express passenger engines, in their final years they were used by Stafford shed on local passenger trains to Wellington and Shrewsbury, along the Trent Valley to Nuneaton and Rugby, and to Birmingham. Here one of the last of the class, No.**25648** *Queen of the Belgians*, poses outside the shed after withdrawal before being hauled away to Crewe

Stafford driver Percy Sams standing beside the old LNWR 'Special Tank' *Earlestown* at the side of the shed in 1949. All of this class had long been withdrawn from normal service, having been introduced in 1870, but a few still survived as shunters at Wolverton Carriage Works. Here *Earlestown* was on its way back to Wolverton after overhaul at Crewe Works. Percy Sams himself retired in 1953.

Don Putman collection.

The next stage in the modernisation of the shed was the rebuilding of No.2 shed, the most noticeable feature of which was the replacement of the roof. Here, Ivatt class '4' 2-6-0 No.**43022** stands outside the shed in June 1949. A batch of these engines, Nos.43020-6, was sent to Nuneaton when first built and regularly worked to Stafford on a morning goods, returning on the 4.35pm local from No.2 bay.

A. G. Ellis collection.

LMS '2P' 4-4-0 No.**40659** on the shed about 1959. This was a long-standing Crewe North engine and had probably visited Stafford with the inspection saloon, a regular job for the Crewe '2P' 4-4-0s. Stafford had its own allocation of engines of this class, notably Nos.40583, 40646, 40678. They were used on local passenger trains to Nuneaton and Birmingham, and also as station pilots after the withdrawal of 40443 and 40461. *John B. Bucknall.*

A general view of the shed in September 1958. On the left is a 'Crab' 2-6-0. Almost certainly it is a Willesden engine and has arrived on an early morning goods, which mainly brought traffic from Willesden yard for South Wales, reaching Salop Sidings about 9.30am. The Willesden men on this turn were not usually asked to do any additional work while at Stafford and just rested before working back to Willesden later in the day, again with South Wales transfer traffic. Next to the 'Crab' are two 'Jubilees', one of them no doubt being rostered to the 3.42pm Salop passenger. *Edward Talbot.*

Busy scene at the north end of Stafford station in the late 1920s. A 'Claughton' is about to depart from the Down platform. Its train has probably been divided and after it has left the 'Prince of Wales' standing on the Down Main line will back down on the portion left behind in the platform. The bay on the left was used for trains on the Great Northern line to Stafford Common, Uttoxeter and Derby - it looks as if a train has recently arrived. An Up local train, probably for Birmingham, is standing at the far end of platform 1 and another 'Prince' is in No.4 bay on the right. On the far right is No.6 signal box and the slow lines. Several workmen complete the busy scene. One of them is standing on the Down Main signal gantry; he is probably the lamp porter, whose job it was to change the oil lamps every day and to keep the spectacles and arms clean.   *S. H. P. Higgins.*

View from the north end of platform 2 on 27th January 1935 as the 'Royal Scot' approaches on the Up Fast line hauled by the first LMS Pacific No.**6200** *The Princess Royal*. The engine is still in original condition with small tender and carries an LNWR-style enamel shed plate '1' (Camden) on the smokebox door. The signalman in No.5 signal box (to the right of the bridge) has already put the signals back to the 'on' position. On the left an Up goods approaches on the slow line hauled by a 'Super D', while further to the left an ex-North Staffordshire Railway tank engine stands beside the shed. The signal is 'off' for a train on the Down Fast line, most probably an express; the other signals on the gantry prominent in the right foreground are for diversions from the Down Fast, from left to right, to the Shrewsbury line, to the Down Slow line and to the Great Northern line. Again, a fascinating and busy scene typical of the steam age.   *P. S. Kendrick.*

Another busy scene at the north end of Stafford station photographed from Bagnall's bridge with a medium telephoto lens. On the left LNER class 'J6' 0-6-0 No.**3623** leaves the Great Northern bay with a local train to Stafford Common and Uttoxeter. An Up goods is standing on the fast line waiting for 'Big Ben' to clear. An LMS '4F' 0-6-0 is performing some manoeuvre between the platform line and the Down Slow, and an ex-North Staffordshire Railway tank engine is standing bunker-first in bay No.4. Probably it has been released, after arriving with a local train from the Potteries, by another engine removing its train, and is now waiting for the road to clear so that it can go to the shed.   *P. S. Kendrick.*

Compared with the view opposite, changes have been minimal since *The Princess Royal* sped through the station some two decades earlier. LNWR semaphores have made way for colour light signalling and flat-bottom rail has replaced bull-head, on the main lines. This 1958 view however is still flavoured with the presence of LNWR built 0-8-0 No.**49357** entering the No.1 platform road on its way to the goods yard. This locomotive was to spend its last years at Stafford shed prior to withdrawal in October 1961.

M.S. Welch.

A very poor picture but one of great interest since it is one of the earliest photographs taken at Stafford. It shows LNWR 'Problem' class 2-2-2 No.**229** *Watt*, the second of the class to be built, at the north end of the station with Railway Street in the background. Probably it was taken in 1862 on the occasion of the high-speed run of the 'Trent Special', which this engine hauled from Holyhead to Stafford and a 'Bloomer' took over for the rest of the journey to Euston. The engine was built before the invention of the injector and relies on pumps driven off the axle to maintain the water level in the boiler - the clack valve on the side of the boiler and the pipes leading to it underneath the boiler can be clearly seen. This picture of course was taken long before the station was rebuilt and enlarged, when there were still only two tracks between Stafford and Crewe.

LNWR Ramsbottom 0-4-0 saddle tank No**3243** standing on the Down Fast line at the north end of the station with Railway Street in the background about 1904. Enginemen were a hardy breed and had to be. It was after the First World War that all LNWR shunting engines began to be fitted with cabs. A night's work on this engine in Salop Sidings in December would test the toughest of men. The engine is on the boarded crossing between the Up and Down sides of the station. Another boarded crossing was provided at the south end. Normally, the lifts and bridge in the middle of the platforms were used to transfer parcels and mail from one side to the other but the boarded crossings were still used occasionally at busy times such as Christmas, or when the lifts were out of order. The south end crossing was so used as late as the 1950s and possibly into the 1960s but the one at the north end had been removed by then. *R. S. Carpenter collection.*

LNER class 'D2' 4-4-0 No.**4320** standing in the Great Northern bay sometime in 1938. It has arrived from Derby at 3.32pm, run round its train and pushed it back into the platform; it will now go to the shed to turn before leaving on the 4.37pm to Derby.   *E. S. Russell.*

Great Northern Railway 2-4-0 No.**78** standing in bay 4 about 1900. Normally this bay was used for local passenger trains to Shrewsbury and Stoke on Trent. So perhaps the Great Northern bay is out of use for some reason such as work on the track or perhaps No.**78** has gone to collect or leave some vehicles.

LNWR 'Jumbo' No.**479** *Mastodon* standing on the Down Fast line about 1920. It was a Stafford engine at one time so it may have just hooked on to a Down express as pilot. If so, it is probably waiting for the other engine to finish taking water.

'Coronation' class Pacific No.**46225** *Duchess of Gloucester* in much the same position as *Mastodon* in the previous picture but some forty years later. The driver is waiting to turn off the water and the fireman will then take out the 'bag' and drop it over the side of the tender. It was unusual for a train to stop for water on the Down Fast line and it only occurred in emergency such as when, for some reason, an engine had failed to pick up enough water at Hademore troughs near Lichfield. This was a Sunday working about 1960 and the troughs were temporarily out of order. It was, of course, more common for this water column to be used by engines standing in the platform. The next set of troughs north of Stafford were at Whitmore.

Edward Talbot.

The down 'Mid-day Scot' passing through the station in 1956 hauled by the only BR standard class '8' Pacific No.**71000** *Duke of Gloucester*. On the right is the water column featured in the previous picture. *Edward Talbot.*

A goods for the Great Northern branch approaching No 5 signal box and crossing from the slow to the fast lines; it has been assembled in Salop Sidings, where it was collected by the two engines, LNER class 'E1' 2-4-0 No.**888** and 'J3' 0-6-0 No.**4151**. The date is 1925.

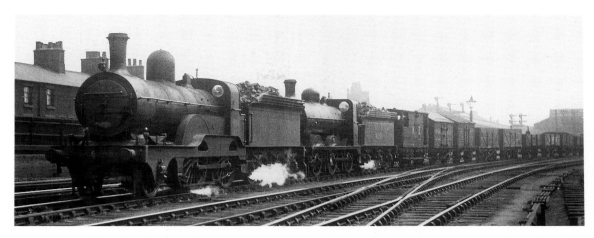

'Rebuilt Royal Scot' No.**46114** *Coldstream Guardsman* leaves the Down platform with a Euston-Liverpool express in 1956. Modern enthusiasts often believe Stanier Pacifics hauled the majority of expresses on the main line in the 1940s and 1950s. In fact there were far too few of them for that and they normally appeared only on certain Scotch and Liverpool trains. The class '7P' rebuilds of the 'Scots', 'Jubilees' and 'Patriots' worked all the other heavy expresses, often with loads of 15 or 16 coaches, and were the mainstay of the line.

Edward Talbot.

An Up goods hauled by Stanier 2-6-0 No.**42983** of '5B', Crewe South shed, approaching the station in the late 1950s. It is crossing from the Up Slow to Up Fast, and the fireman is looking back to check that the train negotiates the crossings safely. The usual crowd of spotters is gathered on the end of Bagnall's bridge.

Edward Talbot.

View of the north west end of the station on 14th January 1960. There are parcel vans in the Great Northern bay, a diesel multiple unit for Manchester via Stoke in the bay on the near side of the station and the stock of a Shrewsbury local in platform 6. On the right are capstans for moving coal wagons to and from the coaling stage. In LNWR days capstans were hydraulically powered but these are electric.

Another view from the same sort of position but a few months later. Part of the roof has been demolished on the Down side along with some of the buildings but the layout has not yet been altered. Stanier Pacific No.**46228** *Duchess of Rutland* waits for the 'right away' in the Down platform, a diesel multiple unit for Manchester via Stoke on Trent stands in No. 4 bay and on the far right is the stock of a Shrewsbury local. *John B. Bucknall.*

View from Bagnall's bridge in the early 1960s during electrification work and the rebuilding of the station. The new slow line platforms are in use but the new station has not yet made much progress and only a few masts have been erected. A Stanier '8F' 2-8-0, No.**48738**, is travelling along the old Down Slow line with a coal train, probably heading for the Shrewsbury line, while a class '5' 4-6-0 is pulling out on the Down Fast with a passenger train from Birmingham to Liverpool and Manchester. Work began on the new station in June 1961. It was opened in December 1962.

Peter Ward.

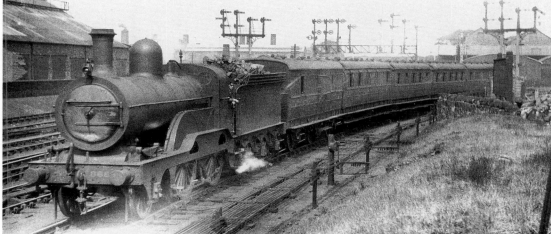

View looking north from Bagnall's bridge and showing the splendid array of signals controlling the northern approaches to Stafford. On the left are the Shrewsbury line signals, in the centre those for the main line and on the right those for the GNR branch. The Great Northern Railway train coming off the branch hauled by 2-4-0 No.**868** is signalled into the GNR bay in the north end of platform 1. On the left is part of W. G. Bagnall's Castle Works. The date is about 1922.

An Up parcels train approaching Stafford on the slow line, also about 1922. The engine is 'Prince of Wales' class 4-6-0 No.**812** *Admiral Jellicoe*. During the First World War the LNWR named a number of its engines after personalities and events made famous by the war.

View taken off Bagnall's bridge about 1927, using a medium telephoto lens which has brought up the signals well to make a dramatic picture. The engine is an unidentified 'Claughton' class 4-6-0 and the train a thirteen-coach Up express. It was standard LNWR practice to have rings on slow-line signals but they were removed early in the LMS period. In the right background is Venables timber yard, and just visible to the right of the engine is a Great Northern signal on a typical concrete post.

P. S. Kendrick.

The signal gantries in the previous pictures were replaced by colour lights in the early 1950s when No.5 signal box was rebuilt in its present location. The view from Bagnall's bridge then remained largely the same until electrification. Here, 'Rebuilt Royal Scot' No.**46151** *The Royal Horse Guardsman* on a Blackpool-Euston express on the Up Fast line passes a diesel multiple unit departing for Stoke on Trent on the Down Slow on 22nd September 1959.

Edward Talbot.

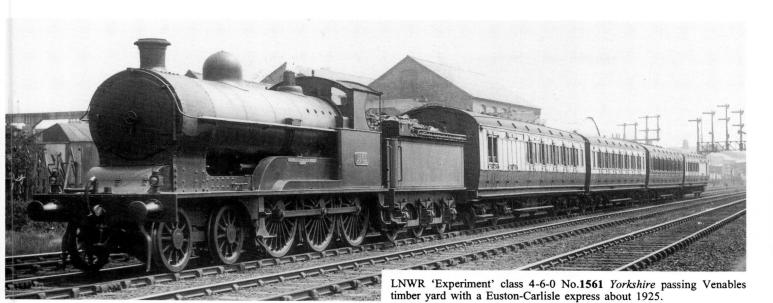

LNWR 'Experiment' class 4-6-0 No.**1561** *Yorkshire* passing Venables timber yard with a Euston-Carlisle express about 1925.

'Super D' No.**49359** of '3A' shed (Bescot) heading north from Stafford with a goods for Crewe on 23rd June 1951. In the distance is the signal gantry controlling the approach to Stafford on the main line from the north. On the right is the Universal Grinding Wheel Company factory and on the left is Venables timber yard. The photograph was taken off Doxey Road bridge.

F. W. Shuttleworth.

View looking south along the Down Fast line under Doxey Road bridge on 11th June 1959. The colour light signals replaced the gantry seen in the previous picture and operated by the old No.5 box. They are LMS type with route indicators.

'Jubilee' class 4-6-0 No.**M5606** *Falkland Islands* approaching Stafford with an Up passenger train on the slow line on 20th June 1948. It is about to pass under Doxey Road bridge. The offices of the Universal Grinding Wheel Company are in the background. The engine is in an early BR livery, which was really an adaptation of the LMS 1946 scheme. It has 'British Railways' in full on the tender and its LMS number is prefixed with 'M' for London Midland Region. This was done for a short time only, until the renumbering scheme for all BR engines had been worked out. The Down Fast has been relayed with flat-bottom rail but the other three tracks are all still laid with bullhead.
F. W. Shuttleworth.

LNWR Webb '5ft 6in 2-4-2 Tank' No.**1393** accelerating away from Stafford near Doxey with what is believed to be a local train for Stoke on Trent. Engines of this class allocated to Stafford used to have a regular working to Liverpool. Because of the distance, they were very carefully coaled beforehand and even had coal stacked on the cab floor.

At first glance a very boring picture. 'Rebuilt Royal Scot' No.**46129** *The Scottish Horse* approaching Stafford with the Llandudno-Euston express due away from Stafford at 12.10pm. It makes the point, however, that the ground north of Stafford is very flat and marshy. The contractors building the line, like Stephenson at Chat Moss, found that it absorbed an enormous amount of filling material before a solid foundation was achieved on which to lay the track.
Edward Talbot.

LMS '4F' 0-6-0 No.**4121** near 'Shaky Bridges' (about a mile south of Great Bridgeford) with a Down goods in the late 1920s.

An unidentified 'Claughton' class 4-6-0 with an Up express on the fast line in the late 1920s. It has just passed Great Bridgeford station, which is in the background on the extreme left.

'Jubilee' class 4-6-0 No.**45588** *Kashmir* passing Great Bridgeford on the Down Fast line on 16th June 1951 with a summer Saturday relief carrying reporting number W99.   *F. W. Shuttleworth.*

Stanier class 5 No.**44971** with self-weighing tender approaching Great Bridgeford on the Up Slow line with a summer Saturday relief to Birmingham New Street on 4th August 1951.   *F. W. Shuttleworth.*

View looking north from the footbridge at Norton Bridge as 'Jubilee' class 4-6-0 No.**45671** *Prince Rupert* approaches on the fast line with an Up express in the early 1960s. Although work has started on rebuilding the station for electrification, the basic layout still remains the same as in late LNWR days. The old signal box is still in use but its replacement has already been completed.
Edward Talbot.

Two views taken at Norton Bridge about 1924 of Mr Walter Reader, one sitting by a North Staffordshire Railway wheel barrow and the other standing by his horse with the LNWR goods shed on the right and the NSR signal box in the background. NSR signal boxes had internal toilets, unlike LNWR boxes where the toilet was downstairs and outside; they also had ceilings, whereas in LNWR boxes there was just the roof rising to its apex. Mr Reader started his railway career as a drayman on the LNWR; his pay was £1 a week. After a time he left the LNWR and went to work for the NSR, also as a drayman, since that company offered him a guinea a week (£1 1s, £1.05). His job entailed taking two dray loads a day from Norton Bridge to Eccleshall, a distance of about two miles. The loads consisted of commodities of all kinds but often included food, beer and spirits, which were conveyed in wooden barrels. A kettle of boiling water poured into an empty whisky barrel on return to Norton Bridge produced a very acceptable drink! *L. W. Reader collection.*

'Coronation' class Pacific No.**46238** *City of Carlisle* on the down 'Caledonian' north of Norton Bridge one summer's evening in 1960.
Edward Talbot.

A heavy Down goods near Badnall Wharf, hauled by an unidentified LNWR '19in Goods' 4-6-0 on 2nd June 1925. These were powerful mixed-traffic engines but being unsuperheated burnt a lot of coal, so much so that they were referred to by some of the men as 'Mankillers'- no doubt the fireman's back is bent in this case too! He will have no opportunity to enjoy the beautiful Staffordshire scenery until they have taken water at Whitmore and are running downhill towards Crewe. The local permanent way gang has also been busy - the tidy paths, hedges and fences are a credit to their efforts, as well as the superb alignment achieved purely by physical effort and without help of machines. This was normal on the LNWR which was always proud of its permanent way. The four-track main line between Stafford and Crewe was its showpiece and was beautifully kept. Today's trains are much faster but the state of the track side is pitiful and indicative of different attitudes.   *courtesy V. Forster.*

When the munitions factory at Swynnerton closed, the sidings at Badnall Wharf were used by Crewe for storing engines which were not needed in traffic, among them some types not normally seen in the area such as Tilbury tanks and Sentinel shunters. Here Sentinel No. **47191** awaits its fate.
                    John B. Bucknall.

General view of engines stored at Badnall Wharf on 27th September 1959. From left to right they are: '3F' 0-6-0 No.**43630**; '1F' 0-6-0 Tank No.**41797**; '3F' 0-6-0s Nos.**43339, 43192, 43313** and **43248**; Sentinel shunter No.**47191**; Compound 4-4-0 No.**41158**; and '3F' 0-6-0s Nos.**43623** and **43318**.
                    F. W. Shuttleworth.

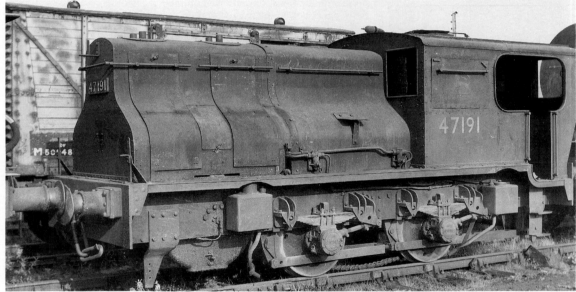

View of Standon Bridge signal box looking south on 9th August 1953.
F. W. Shuttleworth.

Standon Bridge

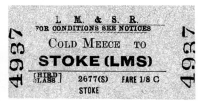

View of Standon Bridge station after closure, looking south from the Up Fast platform and showing the island platform and Down Slow platform on 9th August 1953. *F. W. Shuttleworth.*

The Royal Train leaving Whitmore cutting and heading for Stafford on 5th May 1904. The engines are both 'Alfred the Great' class four-cylinder compounds.   *National Railway Museum.*

An unidentified 'Jumbo' in the cutting south of Whitmore near the end of the climb from Stafford with the 'Irish Day Express', 11am from Euston on 1st October 1900. The load is about 280 tons. It seems incredible nowadays that such a tiny engine could handle such a train. Yet clearly the 'Jumbos' did so regularly and with no particular difficulty. In LMS days they were classified '1P' under the Midland system but few drivers would have relished the prospect of hauling such a train with a Midland engine rated '2P' or even '3P'! The fence on the top of the cutting behind the train was used by Crewe Works for testing different types of paint, which was applied to boards and exposed to the weather. At the top of the cutting side behind the camera was the reservoir built by the LNWR to supply Crewe with water, as the local supplies were inadequate to meet the growing demands when the town expanded rapidly in the middle of the nineteenth century. The site of this reservoir was flattened by bulldozers late in 1989.

The LNWR laid down water troughs at intervals of roughly thirty miles all along the main line. They were sited where ample supplies of suitable water were available, and in any case the supply could be treated, if necessary, to make it suitable for engine boilers. A set of troughs was laid down on the level section just north of Whitmore station. This meant that though Whitmore was at the summit of climbs from both directions, drivers knew they could get water as soon as they got to the top of the bank and need have no worries about working their engines hard. This view shows the north end of Whitmore troughs in 1885

The troughs looking south, as the engines of a Down express take water on the fast line about 1900. The engines are two Webb three-cylinder compounds, 'Experiment' No.1113 *Hecate* and 'Teutonic' No.1304 *Jeanie Deans*.

A race to Whitmore! On the right '6ft Jumbo' No.**635** *Zamiel* is running on the Up Fast line, while on the left 'Problem' class 2-2-2 No.**134** *Owl* is on the slow.

Whitmore

A double-headed Up express on Whitmore troughs in April 1935. The engines are 'Jubilee' No.**5599** and 'Patriot' No.**5521**, which were later named *Bechuanaland* and *Rhyl* respectively. By comparison with the previous pictures, where large ballast is laid down in the space between the tracks, timbers have now been put down, possibly old sleepers, to prevent the ballast being washed away by water spilling from engines. *P. S. Kendrick.*

Only Castle Street separated Stafford engine shed from the Castle Engine Works of W.G. Bagnall, although rail access could only be gained from the Shrewsbury line opposite the Universal Grinding Wheel Co's works. This 1948 (25th August) view shows LNWR built 'Cauliflower' (LMS No.**28345**) being turned against the backdrop of Bagnall's Works. To the right are the offices and stores which were formerly part of the No.1 engine shed.   *W.D. Cooper.*

W. G. Bagnall's Castle Engine Works

Shortly before nationalisation the Great Western Railway ordered 50 '9400' class 0-6-0 pannier tanks from Bagnall's, the order being carried out after the GWR had ceased to exist. Here in 1949 an unidentified member of the class stands in the works yard on completion but before final painting and the fitting of numberplates.

Ken Wood collection.

When work on steam locomotives ceased, Bagnall's built diesels for a while and also tried to obtain other engineering work. The firm built the frames for the first batch of Brush diesels for BR, the 5500 series, now class 31. Here Stafford 'Jinty' No.**47590** prepares to take a train of newly completed mining machinery out of the works. In the background is part of the factory of the Universal Grinding Wheel Company. The engine will draw its train out of the yard and push it across the Shrewsbury line into a siding on the Up side. It will then run round the train and haul it through the station into the yard. On the footplate are driver Fred Davies and fireman Ken Wood.
Ken Wood collection.

In 1952-4 Bagnall's built a new erecting shop. It is seen here with various diesel locomotives under construction for New Zealand in 1955.
Ken Wood collection.

Gnosall

General view of Gnosall station about 1910, looking along the Up platform towards Stafford. Two signals on one post is a typical example of LNWR economy. On the Down platform a porter is hard at work on the station gardens.

View of Gnosall looking towards Stafford along the Down platform in 1949.

(Bottom) Three views of Gnosall, all taken by a local railwayman to show the fine state of the station gardens but also showing incidentally various features of the station.

(centre). Along the Down platform looking towards Newport. The bridge over the Stafford road is at the end of the platform and beyond it is the signal box.

(left). Along the Up platform looking towards Newport.

(right). The exterior of the wooden station building on the Up platform, as seen from the path off the Stafford road.
Malcolm Armstrong collection.

Stanier '8F' 2-8-0 No.**48662** of Shrewsbury shed, passing Gnosall yard with a Stafford-Swansea goods on 18th July 1964. The roof of the station building on the Stafford platform can just be seen above the coal wagons on the right of the picture. *Peter Ward*.

Stanier '8F' 2-8-0 No.**48347** heading for Stafford with a freight from Shrewsbury in June 1963. It is about to pass under the Stafford-Newport road on the west side of Gnosall at a point where the line ran through a beautiful red sandstone cutting. *Edward Talbot*.

Newport

Two views of Newport station, one taken about 1900 and the other about the time of the First World War, both looking west from about the same position. In the later view the platforms have been raised - close comparison reveals other interesting detail changes.
Bernard Matthews collection.

NEWPORT: LNWR.

A Stafford-Shrewsbury local about a mile west of Newport, near the village of Church Aston, hauled by 'Black 5' No. **45190**, a long-standing Shrewsbury engine, in July 1964.   *Peter Ward.*

Towards the end of steam the most unlikely engines were used on work they would never have done previously. For a time a Crewe-London parcels train, which ran via Market Drayton and Wellington to Stafford, was often hauled by a Stanier 'Coronation' class Pacific. Here, in 1964, a 'Britannia' originally allocated to the Western Region, No. **70023** *Venus*, pulls away from Donnington past No. 1 signal box with a three-coach local passenger train to Stafford.　　*Peter Ward.*

Donnington

General view of the Stafford platform at Donnington in 1964.　　*Peter Ward.*

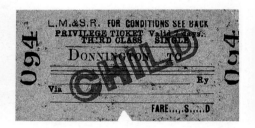

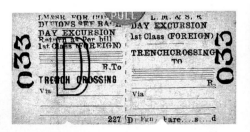

The main station building at Donnington was on the Wellington platform. This view was taken from the steps of No. 1 signal box in 1964.
Peter Ward.

When the 'Jubilees' were displaced from the Midland Division of the London Midland Region, at first partly by 'Royal Scots' and 'Britannias' and then completely by diesels, several of them were sent to Shrewsbury shed and used on the same workings as Shrewsbury's class '5s', over the North and West main line and to Stafford and Chester. Here, one of them, No.45577 *Bengal*, pulls away from Donnington with a Stafford-Shrewsbury local on 3rd September 1964. *Peter Ward.*

When the Standard class '4' 4-6-0s were introduced in 1951, the 75000 series, the first batch was allocated to Shrewsbury shed. Presumably, they were intended for use on turns being performed over the Cambrian lines by ex-GWR 'Manors' from the former GWR shed, as well as on former LMS workings; some appeared at Stafford on local passenger trains. After a time they were largely replaced on the ex-LMS workings by Standard class '5' 4-6-0s, the 73090-9 batch being sent new to Shrewsbury, and Standard '5s' then remained at Shrewsbury till the end of steam. Here, in 1964, No.73026 pulls away from Donnington with a Stafford-Shrewsbury local. Behind the engine is the line to Granville Colliery; it curves round to the right and passes between the gasholder and the houses on the extreme right of the picture to reach the colliery. *Peter Ward.*

Engines from the Western Region shed at Wellington worked regularly as far as Donnington with empties for Granville Colliery and to take loaded coal wagons back to the yard at Wellington. In this 1964 view of Donnington sidings, ex-Great Western pannier tank No.9630 appears to be taking the brake van off the rear of a train of empty wagons, which it has brought from Wellington, before they are worked down to the colliery. On the right is an '8F' 2-8-0 and on the left, in a siding on the other side of the running lines, are loaded coal wagons awaiting removal, probably to Wellington. *Peter Ward.*

LNER class 'J3' 0-6-0 No. 3177 leaving the Great Northern bay at Stafford with a passenger train for Stafford Common, Uttoxeter and Derby Friargate in 1925.

One of Stafford's 'Jinties', No.**47354**, crossing the bridge over the River Sowe en route back from Stafford Common to the main line on 26th February 1963.   *Edward Talbot.*

Stafford Common

GNR 2-4-0 No.**202** at Stafford Common station about 1900. Standing on the left is the first driver on the Stafford & Uttoxeter Railway (as it was before being taken over by the GNR). To his right is his fireman. The engine is fitted with Smith's patent safety chains.

Great Northern Railway 0-4-2 No.**599** at Stafford Common about 1900, with part of the salt works in the background.

LNER 0-6-0 No.**1094** at Stafford Common in 1923. The station is to the right and the trees are bordering on the common from which the station name was taken. Driver Simpson is standing on the running board in front of the cab

LNER 'D2' class 4-4-0 No.**4399** awaiting departure from Stafford Common station with a train to Uttoxeter and Derby Friargate in the late 1920s.
F. W. Shuttleworth collection.

General view of Stafford Common station looking towards Stafford on 18th March 1962.
F. W. Shuttleworth

View inside the wagon maintenance shop at the salt works near Stafford Common station in 1920. There was extensive salt traffic from this branch. The various salt companies had their own wagons, on the sides of which they used to advertise themselves and their products.

(centre-left). A typical wagon used for salt traffic from Stafford Common, in this case by the firm of Chance & Hunt. This picture was taken at the Smethwick works of the Birmingham Railway Carriage & Wagon Company, when the wagon was first completed.

(centre-right). Another salt wagon built by the Birmingham Railway Carriage & Wagon Company for use by a Stafford company. This one was designed to be sheeted over with a tarpaulin, supported by the bar along the top.

Stafford 'Jinty' No.**47354** pauses during shunting operations alongside the signal box at Common station on 26th February 1963. No doubt, the crew have gone for a cup of tea!
Edward Talbot.

LNER 4-4-0 No.**4363** near Hopton on the outskirts of Stafford with a train from Derby and Uttoxeter about 1930. The RAF maintenance unit (16 MU) was built in this area. *P. S. Kendrick.*

There were some quite steep gradients between Stafford Common and Uttoxeter and one tunnel near Bromshall. Here LNER 4-4-0 No.**4353** leaves the tunnel with a train for Stafford about 1930. *P. S. Kendrick..*

At Bromshall Junction trains from Uttoxeter needed to collect the tablet for the single-line section. Here the driver of a Stafford train is climbing down from the engine, LNER 4-4-0 No.**4329**, to go to the box to consult the signalman.

P. S. Kendrick.

The Stephenson Locomotive Society Midlands Area arranged a special train to make 'A Final Run' on the Great Northern line on Saturday 23rd March 1957. It was worked by a push-and-pull set, powered by Ivatt class '2' 2-6-2 tank No.**41224**. The train started from Birmingham and arrived at Stafford on the Down side, from where the station staff wanted it to leave for the branch. The participants, however, wanted to travel over the whole of the branch so far as possible, which included leaving from the Great Northern bay proper; and at the insistence of the organiser, W. A. Camwell, the society's tireless Midlands Area secretary and editor, the train was eventually backed into the bay where it is seen here before departure. *E. S. Russell.*

Chartley & Stowe

On the way to Bromshall Junction, the special train stopped at all stations to allow the passengers to view the remains and take pictures. This is the scene at Chartley & Stowe station. *E. S. Russell.*

The scene at Bromshall Junction before the return run non-stop to Stafford. *E. S. Russell.*

Bromshall Junction

The end of the line. General view of Bromshall Junction with enthusiasts from the last train examining the scene. In the centre foreground, with his back to the camera, is W. A. Camwell himself, photographing the signal box. *Edward Talbot.*